Education Committees

George Cooke
and
Peter Gosden

Councils and Education Press

Published for the AEC Trust by:
Longman Group Limited
Longman House, Burnt Mill, Harlow, Essex, CM20 2JE

c c

First published 1986

British Library Cataloguing in Publication Data

Cooke, George
  Education committees.
  1. School management and organization——Great Britain——History——
  20th century 2. Local government——Great Britain——History——20th century
  I. Title   II. Gosden, P.H.J.H.
  379.1′53′0941   LB2901

  ISBN 0–900313–39–0

Printed and bound in Great Britain by
Biddles Ltd, Guildford and King's Lynn

DATE DUE FOR RETURN

30 JUN 88 8900

21. 03. 88.

21. 03. 88.

30. 08. 88.

11. 10. 88.

10. DEC 91

30 JUN 92

10. FEB 94

This book may be recalled
before the above date

UL 11b

Other publications by Longman Group Limited on behalf of the
Association of Education Committees' Trust:

Learning from Europe

Contents

PART II *George Cooke*

List of Tables

The AEC Trust

Trustees appointed on Charitable Incorporation were:

Chairman
Roland Edward Smith (re-elected 2.11.83) (Former President, AEC and Education Committee Chairman, London Borough of Redbridge)

The Rt. Hon. Edward Baron Boyle of Handsworth (retired 1.2.80) (Former Secretary of State for Education and Science and Vice-Chancellor, Leeds University)

Prof John Race Godfrey Tomlinson, CBE (re-elected 24.11.82) (Director of the Institute of Education, University of Warwick. Former Director of Education, Cheshire. Former President Society of Education Officers.)

Leslie George Bowles, DL (re-elected 11.11.81) (Former President, AEC and Education Committee Chairman, Bedfordshire)

Richard John Laurence Jackson, CBE, DL, JP (retired 4.6.80) (Former President, AEC and Education Committee Chairman, North Riding of Yorkshire)

New Trustees appointed on retirement of former Trustees:

George Venables Cooke, CBE (appointed 1.2.80 and re-elected 11.11.81) (Former Chief Education Officer, Lincolnshire. Former President and General Secretary, Society of Education Officers.)

Hugh Douty, CBE, DL (appointed 4.6.80 and re-elected 11.11.81) (Former President, AEC and Education Committee Chairman, Warwickshire)

Hon. Secretary
The Lord Alexander of Potterhill (Former Secretary, Association of Education Committees)

Hon. Consultant
Sir Roy Harding, CBE (General Secretary Society of Education Officers. Former County Education Officer Buckinghamshire. Former President of the Society of Education Officers)

Foreword

This book explores the development and the achievement of the statutory education committee in England and Wales since it was first established as part of the education system. It seems a timely exercise, for the education committee has gone through considerable vicissitudes in recent years; the signs are that all is not well with the education service and that the role and significance of the education committee need to be reappraised.

It is inevitably a subject in which the AEC Trust has the greatest interest; the Trust like the Association of Education Committees before it has a long sustained belief that the effective distribution of powers in the administration of the education service is an essential condition for freedom in a democratic society. Thus the decision of the Trust to commission a one-time chief education officer and former secretary of the Society of Education Officers, George Cooke, and a distinguished educational historian, Professor Peter Gosden of the University of Leeds, to embark on this book.

It is not a work intended simply to record and observe, however. Its purpose is more positive: to open up discussion at this point in time on how the government of the education service should be best conducted and how the democratic heritage of which the education committee is part can be maintained and enhanced.

Lord Alexander of Potterhill
Secretary
Association of Education Committees' Trust

Councillor Roland Smith
Chairman

Acknowledgements

We have received a great deal of assistance, both singly and jointly, and we wish to place on record our thanks. Mr Vivian Johnston and Mr Peter Morrish of the Brotherton Library, University of Leeds, where the archive of the Association of Education Committees is now housed, have shown their customary forbearance and helpfulness in meeting repeated requests as have the staffs of the Sibthorp Library of Bishop Grosseteste College, Lincoln, and the EMIE and EPIC information services of the National Foundation for Educational Research. We would like to acknowledge the help so willingly given by Mr David Garner, formerly a member of the research staff of the Leeds University School of Education. We are grateful to Lord Alexander, Mr F J Adams, Mr J F Chadderton, Mr D Fisher, Sir Roy Harding and Professor John Tomlinson for reading and commenting on the whole or parts of the text. Their comments have been most helpful; the shortcomings remain the responsibility of the authors. We would like to thank Mrs Jean Maffey and Mrs Anne Perfect for typing our respective parts of the text. Finally we wish to acknowledge the support given by the AEC Trust which has enabled this work to be undertaken.

George Cooke
Peter Gosden

PART 1

Chapter 1

The creation of the statutory education committee

Peter Gosden

Peter Gosden is Professor of the History of Education and Pro-Vice-Chancellor of the University of Leeds. He is the author of a number of works on the history of the education system including The Development of Educational Administration in England and Wales *(1966),* Education in the Second World War: a study in policy and administration *(1976),* The Development of an Education Service: the West Riding 1889–1974 *(with P R Sharp, 1978) and* The Education System since 1944 *(1983). He is joint editor of the* Journal of Educational Administration and History.

School boards

The administration of the maintained education system through local statutory committees dates from the Education Act of 1902. It has been developed and modified partly after debate and discussion through the legislative process but also as a result of changing political and administrative customs and methods in both central and local government.

By 1902 there had already been a good deal of experience of the provision and support of schools through local government machinery; indeed, it can be argued that the education committee as known in the twentieth century was not so much the creation of the

1902 Act as the recognition and formulation through legislation of nineteenth century developments. Before 1870 the provision of elementary schooling had been left to the voluntary agencies encouraged and assisted by grant aid paid directly by the central government. According to its political progenitor, Forster, the Act of 1870 sought merely to 'fill up the gaps, sparing the public money where it can be done without . . .'[1] and doing 'the least possible injury to existing schools.'[2] It would have been possible for the central government to have acted on its own to fill up the gaps. Forster suggested that it would be wrong for the government to attempt this partly because of the sheer administrative difficulties which he thought would arise in an entirely centralised system and partly because it would give too much power to the central administration. Thus local school boards were to be set up where there were gaps in school provision for the purpose of filling them.

The absence of a strong framework of general local government in the nineteenth century led inevitably to the growth of a series of local boards, unions of parishes and so on to deal with specific administrative and social problems as they emerged in an increasingly urbanised and industrialised society. These included water, lighting, poverty, sanitation and elementary education. Essentially Forster's plan was to divide the whole country into districts each of which would be responsible to the central government for its elementary schooling. Forster wrote 'I cannot but think that all hope of success depends on this formation and responsibility of local districts, without which it is hard to see how a national system is possible'. The districts would furnish returns showing the local position and from this the government would assess the number of places needed and the number actually available. Districts would then have the option of meeting the gap in provision by supporting the building of sufficient additional voluntary schools. If they did not follow this course, then each district would have to raise through the rates the sums needed to supply the deficiency.

He felt that in the towns the existing boroughs were the correct unit of population to take as the basis for education districts. Outside the towns either the unions or the parishes might have served, but he believed that the parish was the preferable unit since it was more in accordance with educational tradition and 'less tainted with the idea of pauperism'. On finance, he preferred the rates to a special local income tax and commented that as the existing Treasury grants would continue to be available, the rates and taxes would meet roughly equal proportions of the costs.[3]

The Bill based on these ideas was finally enacted on 9 August 1870, thus opening the way for the first local education authorities.[4] Constitutionally one important difference between these authorities and the committees subsequent to 1902 was that they were directly elected by the ratepayers. The government had originally proposed that school boards should be chosen by town councils in the boroughs and by vestries in the parishes. The change was made by the Commons on a motion by Lord Frederick Cavendish proposing direct election by ratepayers on the single cumulative vote system. This was widely welcomed by free churchmen and other minority groups who believed it would enable them to obtain representation on the boards. The boards were to have between five and fifteen members depending on the size of the population of the particular borough or parish, and each ratepayer had as many votes as there were seats. There were no wards or constituencies and he might distribute his votes as he pleased over the total list of candidates. In practice in the cities the Roman Catholics, for instance, often only ran one candidate and supporters gave him all of their fifteen votes, thereby ensuring they would have a spokesman on the board – not infrequently at the top of the poll in the triennial elections.

The bitterness of the rivalry between free churchmen and the Church of England, between upholders of the board schools and the voluntary schools, meant that any feature in the administrative arrangements might become the focus of contention and this form of proportional representation along with the costs of elections was examined by a select committee of the Commons in 1885. Francis Sandford, Permanent Secretary to the Education Department from 1870 to 1884 and his successor Patrick Cumin both told the committee that they believed the voting system had greatly facilitated the handling of the two main items of business for the boards, school supply and compulsory attendance (the boards enforced attendance at voluntary schools, not simply at their own). Sandford explained that representatives of the religious bodies on the boards had been able to come together and agree on the need for bye-laws enforcing attendance. Moreover where there was a dispute as to whether the need for a new school should be met by a denomination or by the board, this too was usually settled after contention in the local board itself. Comparatively few appeals went to London for settlement, Sandford added, 'we should have been overwhelmed by that work, I think, if the denominations had not been largely represented on the school board'.[5] In view of the renewed concern over the position of parents in school government, it is interesting that Cumin defended the principle of direct election by ratepayers on the grounds that if town councils appointed the boards the members would often be there for all sorts of reasons but 'representatives elected directly by the parents for educational purposes are very superior to any committee appointed by the town council'.[6]

The rural board in a small village where few cared much about education was undoubtedly very weak as an education authority, yet in the cities and towns the boards achieved a great deal. Their clerks were in effect chief education officers; they employed also professional assistants, architects and inspectors. The boards carried out their deliberative functions through well developed sub-committee systems. They built the schools which were required to make elementary schooling universal and they succeeded in enforcing compulsory attendance among many who were not only unused to it but at times even actively opposed to letting their children go to school rather than working to increase the family income.

Technical instruction committees

Towards the end of the nineteenth century the need for a more far-reaching system of multi-purpose local government gained increasing support. The passing of the County Councils Act in 1888 was an important step in this process. The campaign for technical education had led to the Royal Commission which reported in 1884 in favour of greater public support for technical instruction. The Commission proposed that local resources should be expected to provide a large addition to the funds available for technical instruction. In the proposed reorganisation of local government power should be given to the proposed county boards 'to originate and support secondary and technical schools'. The National Association for the Promotion of Technical and Secondary Education served as a powerful pressure group and within a year of the county councils coming into being these pressures led the government to enact the Technical Instruction Bill of 1889.[7] This permitted the new county councils along with borough and urban sanitary authorities to support technical instruction and to raise up to a penny rate for this purpose. This was a weak measure and merely permissive. Liberals and many free churchmen had wished to include school boards among bodies which could supply technical instruction and they were hardly likely to hurry to apply the new measure in areas where they were strongly represented on those local bodies which were given the new powers. Even elsewhere few authorities were likely to hasten to increase the local rates.

But although the Act of 1889 seemed initially to be a slight and not particularly significant measure, it did contain provisions which led eventually to the statutory education committees of 1902. The local authority was permitted to appoint a committee through which it could exercise its technical instruction powers. The Vice-President for Education, Hart-Dyke, explained to the Commons that such a committee would obviously include members of the council to represent the interests of the ratepayers but he hoped it would also include outside persons with a strong interest in technical education. Where an authority took over an existing institution, then that institution should be represented on the committee or, again, if the provisions of the Act were used in the case of a board or voluntary elementary school for the purpose of establishing technical classes, then the managers of the school would be represented on the committee. Even so the actual power of levying a rate or borrowing money would be reserved to the council itself.[8] Thus in this measure were to be found two main features of the principles which were to be associated with education committees in the twentieth century, namely the mixture of councillors and coopted members and the delegation of powers to the committee saving that of rating or borrowing.

These arrangements only began to assume some significance when the Local Taxation (Customs and Excise) Act of 1890[9] offered non-rate aid for technical instruction. The Local Taxation Bill had originally been designed to raise the duty on beer and spirits and to use the funds so raised to compensate publicans whose liquor licences were to be extinguished, to augment the police pensions funds and to distribute to county councils. Under pressure from supporters of the technical education movement, Goschen, the Chancellor of the Exchequer, accepted part of an amendment so that the Act stated that:

> the Council of any such county borough or county may contribute any sum received by such Council in respect of the residue . . . for the purposes of the Technical (including Agricultural and Commercial) Education within the meaning of the Technical Instruction Act, 1889, and may make such contribution over and above any sum that may be raised under that Act.

In the first year local authorities received £743,000. There was still some hesitation on the part of the new authorities to involve themselves in a regular commitment of funds when the grants might turn out to be no more than a windfall. When the matter was raised in the Commons the Chancellor could give no official assurance that the funds would be provided indefinitely, but expressed the personal opinion that 'if county councils set themselves hastily to work, as in many places they appear to be doing, to utilise the grants for important educational purposes it would probably be difficult for any minister to persuade Parliament to divert them, even if he desired to do so.'[10]

The payment of grant encouraged many counties and county boroughs to move into the field of technical education and to make use of the powers granted them in the 1889 Act. The earliest step was to appoint a county technical instruction or education committee. In a number of counties local or district committees were also appointed. While the great majority of county technical education committees had initially only councillors as members, more of them coopted outside members as they became involved in a wider range of activities. In 1895 Devon, Essex, Gloucestershire, London, Somerset, Wiltshire and the West Riding of Yorkshire were coopting non-councillors. A survey undertaken by the Bryce Commission showed that in the West Riding twenty-four members of the committee were drawn from the Council while five members were coopted 'almost entirely for special knowledge'.[11] In Somerset the technical instruction committee consisted of fifteen drawn from the Council, eight were coopted and any urban authority which itself raised a rate of not less than ½d. in the pound for technical instruction was invited to nominate a representative.[12] London technical education board included twenty county councillors and fifteen coopted members. Of the fifteen, two were from the London Parochial Charities, three from the City and Guilds Institute, three from London School Board, three from London Trades Council, one from the Headmasters' Association, one from the NUT and two additional members nominated by the county council. During the next six years four more counties added outside members to technical instruction committees. Huntingdon added no fewer than twenty-seven, nine from school boards, three from grammar schools, one from a minor authority, one trade representative and thirteen others who were simply described as 'educationalists'. The Isle of Ely, Hertfordshire and Norfolk county councils had also put coopted members on their committees.[13] Nottinghamshire and Northumberland were among counties which coopted to sub-committees but not to the technical instruction committees themselves. In the first the sub-committee on agriculture included representatives from the County Agricultural Society and six farmers while the sub-committee on mining included an inspector of mines and a miners' agent.[14]

For various reasons the position in county boroughs was likely to be different. There was unlikely to be the same need for any local district committees even in the largest towns. At the same time the very concentration of varied interests and institutions in the one place facilitated gathering representatives to the main committee. The contrast became clear in the Report of the Bryce Commission for while seven out of forty-nine English counties then had hybrid technical instruction committees, thirty-seven out of sixty-one county boroughs had appointed hybrid committees. By 1902 a further forty-seven county boroughs had hybrid committees, thirteen still confined membership to members of the council while four had never appointed technical instruction committees at all. Although it might be imagined that members of the council would always constitute the majority of members of technical instruction committees, evidence to the Bryce Commission showed that council members were in a minority at Bath, Blackburn, Coventry and Northampton.

Since the areas administered by the council and by the school board were coterminous in county boroughs, it was only to be expected that school board representatives would be drawn on to the council's technical instruction committee. In any case the single school board of the county borough was usually a much more prestigious and influential body than were the numerous medium and small school boards to be found within the boundaries of the typical county. There was, in fact, an agreement at one time between the Association of Municipal Corporations and the School Boards Association that if joint committees were set up they would be constituted on the basis of the council appointing half the members, the school board one third and the remainder being coopted. These proportions were apparently followed in a number of places including Liverpool and Blackburn, but it was also quite usual for the council to appoint a rather larger proportion of the members than the agreement suggested as in Bradford and Bristol.[15] Grimsby was the only county borough where the committee was constituted as a joint committee with half of the members drawn from each body. It was usual in the county boroughs to offer membership of the technical instruction committee to representatives from the borough's grammar school and technical college or mechanics institute. Representatives were also coopted from the main industries, sometimes from the trades council and from local teachers' associations.

Two of the four county boroughs which did not appoint technical instruction committees appear to have refrained for what might be termed reasons of political principle: they were Leeds and Huddersfield. In 1889 Leeds borough council had urged the government to make technical and secondary education the responsibility of the school boards. In that town the school board did operate what were effectively secondary schools as higher grade board schools. Hence in both of these places the full amount of the residue grant was passed over directly each year to certain institutions prominent amongst which were the school boards. In the third of these four boroughs, Northampton, the whole of the grant was passed over to the governing body of Northampton County Modern and Technical School. The council itself appointed five representatives to its governing body. In a similar manner the last of the group, Preston, passed £1,000 of its grant to the Harris Institute each year and the council appointed representatives to its governing body. Preston spent part of its grant under the 1890 Act in reducing the general rate of the town.[16]

Most authorities did delegate all of their powers under the Act of 1889 to technical instruction committees. The delegation of power and the handling of considerable sums of money was obviously a matter likely to involve quite complex administrative issues. The need for a full-time specialist officer to be responsible for this work was most immediately evident in the counties. Where in some of the boroughs much of the grant was passed on to such existing bodies as school boards or technical colleges the need for such an appointment was less urgent. By 1892 thirty-nine counties had appointed directors or secretaries for technical instruction. If technical and secondary education was to flourish, able men were essential in these posts and the National Association for the Promotion of Technical Education urged those counties which had not so far made such an appointment to do so and spoke of the 'wisdom and ultimate economy of offering such salaries as will attract first-rate candidates'.[17]

The National Association arranged a meeting of directors and secretaries in July 1891 to enable an exchange of views to take place and to promote common action. The meeting led to the formation of the Association of Organising Secretaries and Directors for Secondary and Technical Education. By July 1893 sixty counties and county boroughs had appointed education officers and fifty-one of these had joined the Association. The first convener was Macan, the

Organising Secretary for Surrey, and the Association appears to have been mainly concerned with educational questions such as representations to government departments on educational issues, the Society of Arts schemes for examinations in commerce, Science and Art Department grants, the use of London Matriculation results for awarding intermediate (16-plus) scholarships and the organisation of joint scholarship boards and examinations. This Association is the lineal predecessor of the present Society of Education Officers.

While authorities were not obliged to spend the whole of the Residue Grant on education, the great majority did so and by 1900–01 this amounted to just over one million pounds. In the same year £128,000 was raised through the rates. Rates had been levied by 351 out of 1,121 councils with technical instruction powers – while the grant was payable only to counties and county boroughs, non-county boroughs and urban districts could impose a rate for technical instruction.[18]

In the early years there was a tendency in some authorities to support what appeared to be technical education without adequate general educational support. Money was spent on technical or scientific lectures to those lacking the educational standard needed to benefit. Experience led to an increasing realisation of the need to concentrate on more general secondary education and there was an increase in the support offered to existing grammar schools, organised science schools and technical colleges. The form the support for secondary schools took included junior (12-plus) and intermediate scholarships, direct grant aid to institutions was either on a recurrent basis as a contribution towards maintenance and running costs or in the form of special grants for building new laboratories or additional classrooms. By 1899 only seventeen authorities were not operating a system of scholarships and about 5,000 awards were being made annually, half to secondary schools and half to technical and art schools. Another 6,000 or so scholarships were being offered for attendance at evening and domestic economy classes while about 300 awards were being made to students aged 18-plus to attend universities and colleges. The contrast between the most and least active authorities was very marked. London Technical Education Board offered forty 18-plus awards annually. They were worth £60 and fees each year for three years. Herefordshire offered one two-year award annually while Cornwall and Cumberland offered nothing.

London, the West Riding and Surrey probably built up the most ambitious systems of support for technical and secondary education in the 1890s and this involved the development of full systems of sub-committees to handle the work. At its first meeting the London Technical Education Board – as it was called – under the chairmanship of Sidney Webb appointed a special sub-committee to devise a suitable committee system. Apart from its finance and general purposes sub-committee and two sub-committees for individual institutions, the authority set up seven others to cover science classes, art and technology, domestic economy, scholarships, secondary schools, polytechnics, higher education. Thus a strong and centralised system was set up which attracted favourable comment from the Bryce Commission.[19]

The 1902 committees

Its inquiries into secondary education led the Bryce Commission to conclude that there was an urgent need to establish an efficient administrative system if there were to be any hope at all of meeting the nation's need for adequate secondary education. The Commission had found that 'within the same town or district, the local power over secondary education may be shared between a county or borough council, a school board, various governing bodies, managing committees of proprietary schools, local committees under the Science and Art Department, and managers of voluntary schools'.[20] The answer to these difficulties the Commission believed lay in using the county and the county boroughs as the proper unit for local machinery. Towns with fewer than 50,000 had not been made county boroughs under the Act of 1888, they were too small to be regarded as district areas for secondary education and would gain more by forming part of the administrative county in which they were situated. The continued existence of the school boards for elementary education was assumed since it was outside the Commission's terms of reference and separate recommendations were made for constituting the county and county borough secondary education authorities to allow for this. In counties the majority of members should be chosen by the council, of the remainder, one-third (or about one-sixth of the whole) should be nominated by the Education Minister after consulting with any university which had connections with the area, the rest of the members should be coopted by the members already chosen. Thus there might be sixteen from the council, four nominated by the Minister and eight coopted and in this way the representative element might be suitably mixed with those possessing expert knowledge. Rather similar arrangements were proposed for the constitution of authorities in county boroughs with two modifications. Half of the representative majority were to be nominees of the school board while in county boroughs containing a university the one-sixth normally nominated by the Minister were to be chosen by the university.[21]

The need to reorganise, simplify and make more efficient the local arrangements for the administration of education was quickly accepted by the political parties but that was as far as agreement extended. The Liberals and their free church allies were anxious to retain and build on the school board base which had been developed since 1870, the Conservatives were anxious to do all they could to save the Church schools from financial disaster. Following their general election victory of 1895, the Vice President of the Council in the Conservative ministry, John Gorst introduced a bill in 1896 which would have made county and county borough councils authorities for both secondary and elementary schools, paid a special capitation grant to voluntary schools and made denominational instruction available in board schools to those children whose parents desired it. Naturally enough there was strong opposition from the Liberal and free church interests but the bill failed because Conservative supporters from medium sized towns objected to the claims of their towns for education powers being set aside in favour of the counties. The bill was dropped and a short measure was passed in the next year simply to bring financial aid to hard-pressed voluntary schools. The relief proved to be no more than temporary since costs continued to rise and the position of these schools appeared to be even more difficult by 1901.

During his tenure of the office of Vice-President, Gorst's enmity towards the school boards became increasingly pronounced and is reflected in the files of the Board of Education. In 1900 he wrote that there was little point in setting up secondary education authorities in county boroughs unless the powers of school boards were transferred to them since it was not possible to define clearly the separate spheres of elementary and secondary education.

> The school boards have the immense advantage of an unlimited power of rating which the audit of the Local Government Board is quite inadequate to restrain, and are free from responsibility for any other branch of local expenditure . . . I see no prospect of successfully resisting the

design of the school boards in the large towns (1) to give a free secondary education at the expense of the rates, (2) to treat existing educational endowments as mere provision for the relief of rates, and (3) to exonerate all parents who choose to avail themselves of the public institutions of any pecuniary contribution for the higher education of their children . . .

I have never regarded it as possible that school boards could ever be a permanent institution. Like Boards of Guardians they are a modern anomaly in local government which would never have been created if county councils had existed in 1870.[22]

The antipathy which Gorst displayed to the school boards was not simply due to the religious factor but was also clearly social.

It is not necessary to recount again here the detailed events of the political conflict of 1902 and the surrounding years, but a somewhat thrusting and ambitious official, R L Morant, whose political sympathies lay with the government of the day became by far the most important person in the planning of the Education Act of 1902. He was able to find administrative arguments for the political direction in which the government wished to move. He produced an important working paper on the issue of whether to try to build upon, keep and incorporate the boards or whether to abolish them completely. All the points turned in the same direction, abolition.

1   It was impossible to deprive county borough councils of the higher education powers which they had exercised admirably for ten years. Thus if elementary education were to be organised on an *ad hoc* basis it would necessitate separate authorities for higher and elementary education in the larger towns.

2.   But an *ad hoc* authority was in itself a mistake since by making education a separate claim on the local revenues it became in the eyes of local councillors a rival and greedy swallower of the funds which the councillor felt ought to be under his control. By analogy, if a man had two housekeepers, one of whom bought just milk and the other everything else, milk expenditure would obviously come to have a disproportionate share of the weekly monies and the whole economy and health of the household would suffer.

3   The separate elections for boards were a waste of time and money.

4   It was wrong to give a group of people whose main concern was education the run of the public purse. Education fads and extravagancies of all kinds became the normal course of policy with school board members.[23]

The 1902 Act replaced the complex administrative arrangements with full education authority powers for counties and county boroughs. Under pressure from MPs representing towns too small to be county boroughs, municipal boroughs with at least 10,000 and urban districts of 20,000 inhabitants at the time of the 1901 Census were granted powers to administer their own elementary schools under Part III of the Act. It is a matter of some interest now to note that in the London County Council area the boroughs did not gain this power. In a draft clause for the 1902 bill provision was made for the LCC to handle secondary and technical while the boroughs were to take over elementary education. This proposed clause was annotated by Gorst who wrote:

> If the Elementary Education Authority is the County Council their Committee when appointed goes down to the London School Board offices and takes over the whole organisation as a going concern, just as a newly elected School Board has to do every three years. If the borough councils are to be the Elementary Education Authorities provision must be made for dividing the existing school board organisation into 29 separate and independent organisations on some appointed day. Who could do this?[24]

The practical organisational problems of dividing up the education service of central London has since that time more than once caused other reformers to draw back.

The positive reasons for the choice of county and county borough councils as education authorities were for Morant and Balfour part of the case for abolishing the school boards and followed directly from the arguments in the former's *Points against ad hoc*. In a note for Balfour he wrote:

> I suppose we can say that in the county boroughs . . . where the competition between primary and secondary is most flagrant, our Bill *will* set up, simply and effectively, one authority, viz, the town council. Further, that in such non-county boroughs and urban districts as are to be given autonomy for elementary education, the same principle is maintained, since these councils will also have secondary education powers up to a penny rate, and the county council can protect itself against overlapping and competition by its concurrent rating power for secondary over those boroughs and urban districts. While in the great bulk of county areas, as in the county boroughs, there will be literally but one authority – the county council. All this is our great line of defence for compulsorily *abolishing* the school boards. This is the *only* way of getting one authority.

In all the smaller urban areas and in rural districts the county council would become the authority. This meant:

> an absolute departure from the system of 1870, for we immediately set up an authority for every inch of the county for elementary school purposes, and not merely over such portions as cannot provide sufficient school buildings from voluntary effort. In fact, the county council becomes the education authority for the *county as a whole*, not for each parish separately.

Moreover, the note continued, the county would lay down what was to be done in all the elementary schools:

> and the managers of each school, whether rate-built *or not*, will merely carry on the school under those instructions'. The county would have absolute control, 'this must be clearly set out in the Bill; it is of the essence of our scheme. We destroy the school boards, but, in their place we set up an authority with just as real power but with far wider range, for it covers practically the whole country.[25]

Much of this was good material for use by government spokesmen anxious to justify the destruction of the school boards and the extension of rate aid to voluntary schools in the current controversies, but the administrative machinery created by the Education Act of 1902[26] did go a long way to meet the needs described by the Bryce Commission in its Report on secondary education and did give the country a much more unified and stronger system of elementary schools. It became the duty of the new county and county borough education authorities to consider the higher (i.e. other than elementary) education needs of their area as a whole, to take the necessary steps to supply or aid the supply of higher education facilities and to promote the coordination of all forms of education. In the elementary area the new authorities took over all the powers, duties and property of the school boards and took control over all secular instruction in the voluntary ('non-provided') schools. They were to maintain all public elementary schools, provided and non-provided. Thus administrative machinery was created which could meet the repeated criticism of arrangements in the late nineteenth century that while all sorts of educational provision might be made this was undertaken by various uncoordinated and competing agencies and that it was no organisation's duty to take overall responsibility for the adequacy of the services provided in a locality.

If the new authorities were to do what was expected of them, it

was clear from the experience of the technical instruction committees in their early years that a measure of educational expertise
would need to be brought into play. To ensure that this was done,
every authority was obliged to have an education committee to which
every matter relating to the exercise of any education power was to
be referred except for the power of raising a rate or borrowing
money. The council itself was obliged to consider the report of its
education committee before acting save where a particular matter
was urgent.

The composition of the education committee was therefore a vital
question and this was governed by a scheme drawn up by each
authority for consideration and approval by the Board of Education.
The schemes had to follow certain requirements. Normally there
was to be a majority on the committee of members drawn from the
council itself. The council had to appoint persons experienced in
education and persons acquainted with the needs of various types of
schools within its area. This could be done either by selecting
councillors with the right experience or by selecting outsiders; if the
council wished it could invite other bodies to make nominations or
recommendations. The Board advised authorities to allow suitable
local educational bodies either to nominate a member directly or to
recommend a name for the council itself to nominate in filling the
vacancies for coopted members. In a model scheme which it
circulated it set out a list of interests which should always be represented:[27]

– University education
– Secondary education of boys and girls 'in its higher and lower
  grades'
– Technical, commercial and industrial education with special reg-
  ard to local industries
– Training of teachers
– Elementary education in both council and voluntary schools.

Every education committee had to have at least one woman
member and the Act specified that marriage was not to result in
disqualification from membership. The extent to which women had
been drawn into technical instruction committee membership was
shown by a parliamentary return of 1901. Six counties and nine
county boroughs were coopting women under the legislation of 1889
while a further thirteen authorities coopted women to their

sub-committees. But the total number of women members only amounted to 153 for England and Wales. Finally the scheme for an education committee could provide for the appointment of members of school boards in existence on 18 December 1902 as added members of the first committee. The aim was to permit a measure of continuity in elementary education where this seemed to be a desirable way of achieving it. Two or three school board members were often included in schemes for county boroughs but seldom for counties for obvious reasons.

The new arrangements were brought into effect by the new education authorities on the 'appointed day' which for most was 1 April 1903 but a few needed more time to work out their schemes for education committees, get these approved by the Board and have the new arrangements ready to begin operating. The position was different in Wales, but that was due to reluctance to work the new Act for political and religious reasons. The extent to which the Act empowered the Board of Education to amend schemes for committee membership was raised by some authorities and a letter in *The Times* claimed that the wording of the Act on this point was 'directory only not imperative'. A weak reply about this to a question in the Commons by the President of the Board, William Anson, led to a full restatement of the position for Anson's benefit in a minute from the Permanent Secretary. Morant wrote that what must be done was to make 'absolutely and unmistakably clear' that a local authority was not empowered by the Act to make any sort of scheme it pleased and force the Board to accept it. Even where a scheme might seem to fulfil the letter of the Act the spirit and intention behind the Act must also be fulfilled. The Board had a free discretion as a matter of law as to approving or not any scheme. While there were some things which could not possibly be approved in a draft scheme, there were others which the Board could legally approve but in the interests of education was bound almost to insist upon and there were yet other points which the Board might suggest to councils for insertion but which it would not even seek to press.[28]

In its circular guiding authorities on the composition of their education committees, the Board had pointed out that an educational body might lodge an objection to a scheme if it felt its interests were inadequately represented or if the person chosen to represent its interests was not really representative. The Board's enforcement of the Act's requirements along with the experience which some councils had had of the value of coopted members on their technical instruction committees led to the great majority of schemes submitted providing for about two-thirds of the members being drawn from the parent council and one-third coopted from outside interests. Nearly half of the English counties and county boroughs gave the right to nominate three or more members of the education committee to outside bodies. The others met the requirements of the Act by first consulting and seeking suggestions but themselves making the nominations.

As a large authority with a multiplicity of interests Lancashire arranged to coopt from most of the education groupings to be found among the added members of committees nationally. They included two university representatives, one from Liverpool and one from Manchester, three from Church of England school associations, two from Noncomformist organisations and one each from the Roman Catholic association, secondary school teachers, elementary school teachers, the Association of Lancashire non-county boroughs, the Royal Lancaster Agricultural Society and Wigan and District Mining and Technical College. For the first year there was a representative from the existing school boards.[29] Representative members from the churches with their large stake in the voluntary schools were perhaps the largest and most usual group among the coopted members in most authorities. Representatives of the teachers were to be found on many education committees but were by no means as general as those from churches. Representation from the county association of non-county boroughs had its parallel in a number of other counties which had several Part III authorities. At the same time the education committee schemes of some Part III authorities reflected a degree of reciprocity. Those in Lancashire seem normally to have provided for one or two added members from the county council. In the South such Part III authorities as Dover and Rochester provided places for Kent County Council nominees, Salisbury and Swindon for Wiltshire and Taunton for Somerset County Council nominees. This cross-representation between Part II and Part III authorities represented a sensible attempt by those responsible for higher and elementary education respectively in the same town to work together and it was the policy of the Board of Education to encourage this in an attempt to overcome some of the problems inherent in having two education authorities in one town.[30] The schemes for education committees in the Part III authorities did not differ in principle from those in counties and county boroughs. The committees were often smaller and added members were coopted from fewer organisations. The most regular feature was again the cooptation of representatives of the three main church groupings to the education committee.

Representation beyond these categories and the actual manner laid down in schemes for coopting the added members depended greatly on the history and traditions of particular localities and bodies. There was something of a regional difference of approach in the schemes submitted. In the twelve county boroughs south of a line from London to Bristol there were only thirteen committee members nominated by outside bodies. But the twenty-two county boroughs in Cheshire, Lancashire and Yorkshire had 142 members nominated by outside bodies or an average of between six and seven members per authority against one in the southern authorities. A similar contrast existed between the counties in the south and the north. Presumably the foundation and growth of university colleges, mechanics institutes and technical schools and colleges in the industrial towns of Yorkshire and Lancashire in the nineteenth century meant that the technical instruction committees in the 1890s and the counties and county boroughs after 1902 were entering an area which already had institutions and organisations created by local initiative to meet the industrial and commercial needs of the rapidly growing communities of Victorian England. Industrial and commercial development in the southern towns and counties had been on a different scale and often different in nature and it had not therefore produced the same proliferation of educational bodies and institutions.

The hybrid statutory education committee of the 1902 Act was created as a result of the experience of the technical instruction committees. In the light of this it was not judged feasible to hand over the education service to the multi-purpose local authorities to be run through an ordinary council sub-committee since the interests involved were much too complex. Many religious and other groups had a stake in the local education arrangements and they had to be brought into the local government of education if the system were to have a chance of operating smoothly. They could not be simply shut out.

The transition to the new committees was eased by the fact that many of their members had been members of the pre-1902 committees or boards in both counties and county boroughs. In the West Riding, for instance, twenty-seven of the thirty-six council members who sat on the first education committee had been members of the last technical instruction committee. Five of the seven men coopted from outside the council had served as coopted members of the last technical instruction committee. The sub-committee lists also showed a marked degree of continuity of individual membership among both elected and coopted members.

In a similar way the transition was greatly facilitated by the growth of a body of experienced local education administrators in the counties and county boroughs in the 1890s and in the larger school boards. Many of the post 1902 education authorities already had competent and knowledgeable men as secretary for or director of technical education and these quite often filled the new post of director of education. This did not always happen and in Leicestershire, for instance, one of the best known directors of education of the first half of the twentieth century, William Brockington, came to the post from the principalship of the Victoria Institute in Worcester in response to an advertisement – the county council preferring to do this rather than appoint the secretary of their existing technical instruction committee. At the same time Leicester county borough council more typically appointed the existing chief officer of Leicester School Board as its new director.[31] Manchester county borough was unusual in not even moving to one director. The former director of technical education became director of higher education while the secretary to the school board became director of elementary education. Only on the retirement of the former in 1911 did Wyatt, director of elementary education, become simply director of education and bring the two sections of the education department together.[32] As might be expected, the counties tended to have former technical instruction committee officers as directors while the position in county boroughs was more mixed and quite often the secretary to the school board became director.

References

1 Hansard, HC, CXCIX, 3rd Series, Cols. 443–4, (17 Feb. 1870).
2 PRO, ED 24/2, Memorandum of suggestions for consideration in framing the education bill, 21 Oct. 1869.
3 Ibid.
4 33 and 34 Vict., c. 75.

5   Select Committee on School Board Elections (Voting) 1885, QQ.7–32, Evidence of Sandford.
6   Ibid., Q.696, Evidence of Cumin.
7   52 and 53 Vict., c. 76.
8   Hansard, HC, CCCXXXIX. 3rd Series, cols. 158–91 (1 Aug. 1889).
9   53 and 54 Vict., c. 60.
10 National Association for the Promotion of Technical and Secondary Education, *Fourth Annual Report*, July 1891, p. 9.
11 Royal Commision on Secondary Education, 1895, Minutes of Evidence, Q. 14,420.
12 Ibid., Q. 3278.
13 P.P. LXXX, 1902, Return showing the number and composition of technical committees in counties and county boroughs, pp. 541–56.
14 *The Record*, IV, 18, p. 173.
15 *County Council Times*, 10 Mar. 1900, p. 132.
16 P.P. LXXX, 1902, Return showing the extent to which and the manner in which local authorities . . . have applied funds to the purposes of technical education.
17 National Association for the Promotion of Technical and Secondary Education, *Fifth Annual Report*, 1892.
18 Ibid., *Fourteenth Annual Report*, 1903, p. 31.
19 Royal Commission on Secondary Education, 1895, *Report*, p. 37.
20 Ibid., p. 65.
21 Ibid., pp. 267–70.
22 PRO., ED 24/29, Gorst to Devonshire, 13 Dec. 1900.
23 PRO., ED 24/14, Points against AD HOC, R.L.M. undated.
24 PRO., ED 24/18, Notes on Draft for Bill, J Gorst, 8 Jan. 1902.
25 Ibid., Morant to Balfour, 3 Jan. 1902.
26 2 Edw. 7. c.42.
27 Board of Education, Circulars 470 and 470B, Feb. 1903.
28 PRO., ED 10/98, Morant to Anson, 26 Apr. 1903.
29 PRO., ED 139/102, Establishment of education committees, Lancashire County Council, 5 Feb. 1903.
30 PRO., ED 10/158, LA Selby-Bigge to President, 12 Nov. 1913.
31 Malcolm Seaborne, 'William Brockington Director of Education for Leicestershire 1903–1947', *Education in Leicestershire 1540–1940* (ed. Brian Simon), pp. 195–6.
32 SD Simon, *A Century of City Government*, p. 262.

Chapter 2

Education Committees in the early decades of the twentieth century

The question of devolution

A fundamental distinction between local government bodies in this country and those in many other European states and North America lay in the much more limited nature of their authority. In the latter local authorities could in general do anything for the good of their district which the law did not actually forbid them to do and for which they could raise the necessary resources. In this country local authorities could only undertake such functions as they were empowered by statute to handle. The statutes themselves have often required the prior consent of a government department to the exercise of particular powers and have authorised government departments to make orders and regulations by which the manner of their exercise might be prescribed or to attach conditions. Yet, although in theory English local authorities might have had less scope than by custom existed elsewhere, in practice, provided they remained within their powers, they were not subject to central control and the decision as to whether they were remaining within their powers lay with the law courts not the central government.

Thus while the statutory education committee had the right of considering and reporting to its council on all matters relating to the exercise of the council's educational powers and of having its report considered before the council could take action, the particular arrangements made for the exercise of these rights varied a good deal from one place to another. The education committee normally exercised extensive powers of action delegated to it by the council. The action taken was reported in due course to the council for information but it was entirely valid without the councils' approval. The crucial factor was the precise form taken by the standing orders of each council where the terms of delegation were laid down. Many county councils only met quarterly and in these authorities any considerable reservation of administrative decision or action to the council would clearly have caused impossible delays and so the delegation of powers to the education committee was extensive or even complete within the limits of the approved estimates. In many urban areas there was a similar delegation of powers to education committees.

While the Education Act of 1902 did in fact prove to have settled the general pattern of local educational administration for much of the twentieth century, it was by no means obvious that this was going to be the position in the years immediately after 1902. The larger county authorities seemed to many to be particularly unsuitable and the Education Bill introduced by the Liberal government in 1906 sought to reform local educational administration as well as to change the denominationally controversial 'dual system'. In the words of a confidential memorandum in the files of the Board of Education 'By the abolition of school boards the Conservative government dealt a death-blow to local public control over provided schools in county districts. A bit of county administrative machinery was substituted for the responsibility of ratepayers – many of them parents of children in the schools.'[1] The memorandum went on to cite with approval James Bryce's opposition to the proposed statutory education committee in the 1902 debate. He objected to it on the grounds that 'it stood apart from the people, is never subject to popular election, is not amenable to the vote of the people, never explains and can never submit its policy to the people and can never have that stimulus and strength which contact with popular opinion gives to an elective authority'.[2]

The Bill of 1906 proposed that an urban district or a non-county borough with a population of at least 50,000 could apply to the Board to be taken out of the jurisdiction of the county council and itself to become an authority for higher education. In elementary education boroughs, urban districts, rural districts and parishes or any combination of them were to be able to apply to take over the management of schools in their areas although the county council would continue to have some financial responsibility for the schools. Schemes for delegation were to be submitted for approval to the Board of Education and that body was to grant approval if the appropriate procedures had been followed.

County councils strongly opposed the proposals. Henry Hobhouse, a leading figure in the former technical instruction committee and then in the education committee of Somerset, wrote to Birrell, President of the Board, putting the County Council Association's (CCA) case that the Bill would 'hopelessly dislocate and interfere with the present organisation without putting any satisfactory system in its stead'. He feared that the councils of smaller parishes would normally claim the right of management solely with a view to saving the rates. This would reproduce the problems of the small school boards without their advantages for few would contain any educationalists.[3] In subsequent discussions between the government and the CCA no agreement could be reached. The papers make clear the continuing objection of some Liberals to any non-elected i.e. coopted members on education committees. Morant, the permanent secretary, could hardly have been serving his current masters in a single-minded manner when he wrote of the liberal leaders to Hobhouse that 'We found they were all over the place amongst themselves when we put really testing questions to them'.[4]

The smaller authorities naturally supported the administrative proposals in the Bill. The executive committee of the Association of Education Committees (AEC) – the formation of which is described on page 26 – had in fact proposed to the Board of Education that places with a population of 50,000 or more should have the right to assume the same powers with regard to higher education as county boroughs. Clause 25 embodying this had indeed been inserted by Birrell as a result of the Association's representations.[5] Many of the urban authorities wanted to go further and at its annual general meeting the AEC resolved that the Bill should be amended to allow adjacent borough or urban district councils with the necessary combined population to approach the Board for recognition as one authority for both higher and elementary education.[6]

The Education Bill of 1906 failed – as did all other attempts by the Liberal government to reverse the denominational settlement of

1902 – largely because of the power of the denominationalists in the Lords and no change was therefore possible in the administrative structure. In immediate retrospect the view in the Board of Education was that the difficulty was to reconcile the points of view of the county councils who naturally resented any breaking up of the administrative organisation which they had created with considerable effort since 1902 and which was in many counties beginning to work smoothly, and of a strong body of Liberal members and administrators who disliked the excessive centralisation which the Act of 1902 had produced in the rural districts and who regretted the loss of the old *ad hoc* authorities with their frequent accompaniment of local enthusiasm for education.[7] In April 1907 the Board asked its Consultative Committee with the Liberal educationist AHD Acland[8] as chairman to look at this matter and to consider what methods were 'desirable and possible' under existing legislation for securing greater local interest in the administration of elementary education in the counties by devolution or delegation of powers and duties to district or other local committees.

The Consultative Committee reported in the following year. Its main conclusion was that it would be difficult if not impossible to devise any uniform system of devolution which every county authority could be obliged to adopt. The committee found that of sixty-one counties, thirty-two had appointed district sub-committees of one sort or another to which some powers had been devolved although twelve of these had only devolved powers in connection with school attendance. In the other twenty counties powers varying greatly in extent and character had been devolved to specially formed district sub-committees. Some of the sub-committees consisted entirely of members of the county council and county education committee while others consisted of combinations of these members with representatives of urban and rural district councils or managers of schools, perhaps with added nominated or coopted members. At the other extreme the Consultative Committee reported that in twenty-two counties the only form of devolution lay in granting various degrees of freedom to individual bodies of managers. There was no link between the level or type of devolution adopted and the general condition of education in each county.

In the light of these findings, the Consultative Committee went no further than to advise the Board of Education to recommend to counties which still had entirely centralised systems to study the returns from devolved administrations which the Committee included in its Report so that they could see which forms of devolution had been effective and to consider whether any such schemes could be successfully adopted in their own areas also. It also pointed out that devolution to a local body would be likely to be successful only if important and interesting duties were delegated to it and if it were given considerable executive power to carry out the duties. The arguments advanced in favour of more devolution were that it stimulated local interest and support for education, that it gave the counties the benefit of local advice and that the central office could be relieved of cumbersome detail. The arguments against devolution were that it added to administrative costs and that it complicated administrative arrangements unnecessarily.

Against this background no new legislative requirement for schemes of devolution was undertaken until these issues came to be reconsidered when Part III authorities were abolished in the 1944 Act and divisional executives were set up in certain areas. In some of the larger counties within which were several medium sized towns where responsibility for elementary education lay with Part III authorities, district committee systems could help to prevent the policies for secondary and elementary education from drifting too far apart. The position between the two world wars in counties with concentrations of Part III authorities was that in Kent there were 24 district committees, in the West Riding 112, in Lancashire 34 for elementary and 100 for higher education and in Middlesex 13 for higher education.

Local authority associations and relations with the Board of Education

The administrative arrangements from 1902 produced local education authorities of very different sizes and capacities even within the same legal and administrative category. At the time of the 1921 census the administrative counties varied from Rutland with 18,368 inhabitants to Lancashire with 1,746,139 or London County with 4,483,249. The size of populations in county boroughs varied from 23,738 in Canterbury to 919,438 in Birmingham. Among Part III authorities Tiverton with 9,715 inhabitants contrasted with Willesden which had 165,669. On grounds of population alone some of the bigger Part III authorities might have had a better claim to run their secondary schools than some of the smaller counties and county boroughs which had been given Part II (higher) as well as Part III (elementary) powers. These wide variations in size need to be born in mind when considering both the degree of cooperation and the conflicts of view and of interest shown by local education authorities in providing an education service and in developing their relationship with the central government.

Coming together to discuss common problems had been the accepted practice among many of the school boards until 1902 and they had a standing organisation – the School Boards Association – for that purpose and for representing their views to the government. Many of the new urban LEAs after 1902 were coterminous with the school boards which had preceded them. Thus the custom of meeting together and forming an association was hardly new in 1903 and an 'informal' conference of a number of education authorities was held at the Holborn Restaurant in London on 10 February 1904. The education committee of Leicester county borough had convened the meeting and the then Mayor of Rochdale proposed the motion that a sub-committee should be appointed to consider a possible scheme of organisation for an association of education committees. When the sub-committee met the next month, one member – the town clerk of Accrington – questioned the wisdom of forming any organisation outside the Association of Municipal Corporations (AMC) but the other members believed there was an urgent need to form an association 'for educational purposes alone'. The majority view was expressed by the *School Government Chronicle* which pointed out that the tasks delegated to education committees by statute were of such a magnitude that an independent central association rather than a mere sectional committee was essential for the proper coordination of the work of education. Moreover it was hoped that all education committees would eventually join and that would obviously not have been possible through the AMC.

The first annual general meeting of the Association of Education Committees was held in October 1904 and the first President, Tudor Walters, stressed that ideally the AEC should represent committees from all areas, large and small, rural and urban. Party politics were irrelevant to the work of the Association whose object was to do the best it could 'to put within the reach of the children of this country the best possible education that could be afforded them.'[10] There was no feeling of enmity towards other organisations such as the County Councils Association, the President said. The membership by the autumn of 1904 however did not include any county education committees. There were 50 county borough committees, 69 non-county boroughs and 41 urban districts, 160 committees in all representing a total population of about ten millions. The Annual Report for 1904–5 regretted that the counties had not so far joined the Association even though their problems were in many ways similar to those of the boroughs, 'unity of action could only be helpful to the cause of education'.[11] The number of education committees in membership was to grow steadily. In 1907 there were 57 county boroughs, 69 non-county boroughs and 36 urban districts, a total of 162. By 1910 the total had reached 173 although there were still no counties.

The main effort of education committees in the first decade of this century lay in bringing together in a system the variety of school board and voluntary elementary institutions for which they had become responsible. In the case of Part II authorities, provision also needed to be made for secondary and technical education even though the Education Act of 1902 merely conferred powers to act in these matters rather than an obligation to do so as in elementary schooling. All of this work was bound to lead to increasing expenditure and the financial problems associated with their efforts to bring together local systems of education dominated the thoughts of many education committees and of local authority associations in the early years. The local authorities were faced with growing costs without any commensurate increase in government grant. The effects were twofold: the proportion of educational expenditure falling on the rates increased while educational development itself was retarded. The President of the AEC went so far in 1907 as to claim that the elementary side which had made very satisfactory advances in the late nineteenth century had not merely ceased to make progress but had retrogressed whilst even the Board of Education had described the secondary side as in a state of chaos.[12] Perhaps Morant, the permanent secretary, would not have found this surprising since he had advocated the 1902 local government arrangements and the abolition of *ad hoc* authorities precisely on the grounds that educational expenditure would be checked by making 'all education part of the ordinary municipal purse'.[13]

In November 1908 a deputation from the AEC to the Chancellor of the Exchequer, Lloyd George, to seek more government aid had returned from their meeting with little more than sympathy. He had pointed out that the ratepayer and the taxpayer was often the same man and even if he was to give larger grants from the Exchequer the ultimate burden would fall on much the same people. Education committee members were not convinced by such reasoning. At a time when the Board of Education was increasing the demands made on local authorities and implementing national schemes which cost money – such as medical inspection and meals for necessitous children – it was for the government to provide additional resources. In 1901–02 government grants covered 58 per cent of educational expenditure; eight years later this proportion had fallen to 50 per cent. In 1911 the AEC considered inviting the education committee of the CCA to form a joint committee to approach the government on the financial issue. It felt unable to work with the AMC since that body only looked at matters from the ratepayers' point of view regardless of the interests of education – indeed the AMC had passed a resolution in 1904 saying that the AEC was unnecessary and this attitude of hostility had persisted.[14] Apart from the counties a few of the biggest county boroughs including Birmingham, Liverpool and Manchester remained outside of the AEC. In 1911 representatives from Leeds proposed at an AMC meeting that steps should be taken to secure the disbandment of the AEC since, they claimed, there was no evidence of any need for its continued existence.

The large, non-associated, LEAs themselves pressed for a Council of Education and at a meeting held in Manchester in 1911 representatives of Birmingham, Manchester, Liverpool, Lancashire and the West Riding agreed a statement which made it clear that the financial burden was foremost in their minds in making such a proposal. 'In the forefront of questions demanding consideration must be placed the necessity for changes in the incidence of local and imperial charges for the cost of education. The present inequalities undoubtedly fetter the spread of educational facilities, make the cause of education itself unpopular, and prove an impossible barrier to progress in many parts of the country'. The statement proposed that the Council of Education's members should be appointed by the councils themselves, not by education committees, and that only members of the councils should be eligible – coopted members of the statutory education committees were to be excluded.[16]

Proposals to bring together representatives of councils rather than of education committees were hardly likely to appeal to those in membership of the AEC and that body wrote to the group representing the large authorities stating that while it supported proposals for joint action in dealing with the Board of Education, it believed that the objective should be to achieve a consultative committee representing the existing education associations.[17]

The departure of Morant from the post of permanent secretary and his replacement by Selby-Bigge led to a much more sympathetic and understanding attitude on the part of the Board. Both LEAs and teachers' associations seem to have found Morant rigid and over-bearing and his method of working helped to produce the sense of injustice which both authorities and teachers came to exhibit in those years for ostensibly different reasons. Selby-Bigge made a point of emphasising the importance of the concept of a partnership between the Board, LEAs and teachers with each playing their part in in-fluencing the development of the education system.

In December 1911 Selby-Bigge sent a minute to JR Pease, then President of the Board, outlining what he thought the Board's attitude should be to the requests for consultative machinery. The Presidents' constitutional responsibility as a minister precluded the surrender of any powers to a statutory committee. He admitted that while the CCA, AMC and AEC were all 'very estimable bodies' 'either through their fault or ours they have not been very useful or effective for purposes of consultation'. A really representative body for rapid consultation would be valuable but there was little hope of getting one because of the divergence of interests, of educational standards and general attitudes towards education, the differences of size and of financial resources 'between London at one extreme and Rowley Regis at the other' would make it very difficult indeed to get a body that could be representative of all, or even of all the most important, LEAs. He explained that he was himself 'a very strong believer in the advantages of taking LEAs into our confidence before making administrative changes of importance . . . I think we do really want to know how our proposals appear to LEAs from their own point of view'. He concluded that in view of the problems associated with creating new machinery he felt 'rather prejudiced in favour of more extensive direct consultation'.[18]

Further correspondence and internal minutes on the files of the Board of Education show that Pease and Selby-Bigge maintained their opposition to any statutory body on the grounds that a minister must bear the responsibility for his department in the face of the statutory concept being pressed by the Liverpool-Manchester con-ference of authorities. Moreover they were both opposed to a repres-entative council of LEAs as conceived by that conference since it was 'only too likely to be nothing better than a glorified ratepayers' association if it is confined to members of LEAs with a warlike official as its secretary' – as Selby-Bigge put it. He also suggested to

Pease that the people who would be put on the proposed council would be of

> the least assistance to us in discussions of the pros and cons of educational administrative proposals, and, of course, they will concentrate against us all the forces of the opposition on financial grounds and if they can in any sense claim to speak for the whole body of LEAs even in this respect it would be much more difficult to defeat the backward and parsimonious LEAs in detail.

If coopted educationists and officers were excluded and the proposed council were confined to members of local authorities, it was very unlikely that the members of such a council would possess the detailed and technical knowledge needed in consultations.[19]

Later in 1912 James Graham, director of education for Leeds, pressed on the Board the view that the AMC and CCA should get together from time to time to serve as the consultative council. He told Selby-Bigge in an interview that the LEAs proper (i.e. the borough and county *councils*) were fully represented by these two organisations and that the AEC was no more than a survival of the old Association of School Boards. The notes on the meeting show that Selby-Bigge responded with the comment that the education committees of the AMC and CCA 'have not been of much use to us up to the present' and went on to suggest that Graham's proposal would produce little more than another ratepayers' association. He added that the smaller authorities and the AEC could not be ignored in any future arrangements.[20]

Correspondence with Tudor Walters, the first president of the AEC and at this time a member of Parliament, shows that he and other influential members of that Association had decided to try to draw the remaining large urban authorities into membership so that it might become fully representative of urban education committees. By April 1913 Tudor Walters was able to report to the AEC Executive that a further seventeen education committees had joined the Association and that these included Birmingham, Liverpool and Manchester. But by 1913 there were difficulties with the CCA which feared that urban areas would possess an undue share of representation in the proposed national council.[21] By the time the First World War began there was still no sign of any generally acceptable arrangement for a council. In 1912 Selby-Bigge had commented that the difficulties were largely due to the jealousy of the existing associations and of some of their members and that may well have been the main reason for the failure of the pressure for a consultative body.[22]

If it had proved impossible to establish any single statutory or consultative council for education, the Board of Education certainly showed a willingness to consult with local education authorities to a much greater extent than in the first years of the century. Both JA Pease, and Selby-Bigge visited the annual general meeting of the AEC in 1913 and the comments Pease made in his speech on local authority associations are, perhaps, worth citing:

> if anyone were to ask me why I am so delighted at the opportunity of congratulating you as an Association of Education Committees when, at the same time, we have in existence Associations of County Councils and Municipal Corporations, I would say that these latter bodies look at education from a somewhat different standpoint to the experts who are meeting together in association in this hall. Local authorities have a large number of other interests and, I must admit, often to my own boredom, that when I meet them they will not talk to me about education, but they will always represent the interests of the ratepayers rather than face the educational problems with which you, as a body, are brought into daily contact.[23]

The financial pressures which lay behind much of the demand by LEAs for closer consultation were reflected in the arguments for more government funds for education which Pease put to his colleagues in the government towards the end of 1913. Quite apart from the demands thrown up by the reorganisation of education after 1902, there had been a growth of other forms of local authority expenditure. Net expenditure of six main services had risen from £33,000,000 in 1901–2 to £55,000,000 in 1911–12; of this latter expenditure on education amounted to nearly £29,000,000 or more than half of the total. The Treasury had set up a departmental committee (the Kempe Committee, so-called after its chairman) in 1911 to review the problem of financing education and certain other services. It was in part with an eye to pressing on his government colleagues the need to meet the increased expenditure likely to arise from the committee's recommendations that Pease circulated his memorandum in December 1913.[24]

The Kempe Committee recommended that the 1888 system of assigned revenues should be abolished and that in future all state assistance to local authorities should take the form of direct grants from the Exchequer and that these should only be made in respect of 'semi-national' services – services which were administered locally 'yet partake somewhat of the characteristics of services administered by the state'. The formula for calculating the grant for elementary education for each authority was 36 shillings per pupil in average attendance plus 40 per cent of the net expenditure less the product of a seven penny rate over the area of the authority. This last was intended as an equalising element between areas of high and low rateable values. No area was to receive more than two-thirds of its net expenditure by way of grant if the balance of expenditure falling on the rates would be reduced below a shilling rate. In more general terms the Committee justified its recommendations on the grounds that no reform could attain any degree of permanance unless it provided for 'an automatic expansion of the government grant concurrently with an increase in the local expenditure which it is intended to aid'. The semi-national services were an integral element of national finance. The Kempe Committee also stated that one of the advantages of a system of grants based upon expenditure was that it would tend to increase parliamentary control over the expenditure of local authorities on semi-national services.[25]

These recommendations were generally welcomed by education authorities. The reactions of individual authorities depended upon the extent to which the detailed application of the proposed formula would suit their particular circumstances and give them more money. There were differences between large and small, urban and rural authorities. When the matter was considered at its annual meeting by the AEC, after a good deal of discussion the members resolved that 'the Kempe proposals established recognition of the important principle that government grant should increase automatically with local expenditure, and this Association, therefore, approves broadly of the Kempe proposals as the best means of distribution of the fixed sum incorporated in the expenditure for the years 1914–1915 (part) and 1915–1916'.[26] Although the Finance Bill of May 1914 promised fulfilment of the Kempe proposals, the necessary procedural changes had not been enacted before the war began. There was some hope of incorporating the new grants in wartime measures in 1915 but the replacement of Pease by Arthur Henderson when Asquith formed a coalition government in May of that year effectively ended hopes of immediate realisation of the new scheme[27] and it eventually came to form part of the post-war reconstruction.

The AEC, the Burnham Committees and the Fisher Act

The greater ease of consultation between education committees and the Board led to consultations with the authorities' organisations and especially with the AEC both with regard to current difficulties and over planning for post-war reconstruction. Alderman Kenrick of Birmingham in proposing the adoption of the annual report at the AEC's general meeting in 1915 thought it worth commenting on the 'most amicable character' of relations with the Board of Education. The Board for its part was said to have found it worthwhile to submit its plans and schemes for comment to the AEC before acting. Kenrick assured his colleagues that the permanent secretary had commented to him on how well consultative arrangements were working and that the only cause for regret was that they had not been adopted earlier. The arrival of HAL Fisher as President of the Board in 1917 was particularly welcome to the AEC and Tudor Walters speaking of the President's maiden speech in the Commons found in it 'an atmosphere of culture and breadth of view, of grasp of problems and conception in the work we have to do that I am bound to say filled me with high hope and ardent expectation.'[28]

By this time the great majority of all education committees were members of the AEC. The Association now had 204 members out of 318 committees and within this total were 75 county boroughs but few county council committees. Writing a few years later, Selby-Bigge referred to the local authority associations generally and the AEC in particular as most valuable agencies for consultation as manifold issues were connected with legislation, finance, regulation or administration. For some time the Board's view had been that the stronger and more coherent these associations were, the better for the Board itself and for the education service as a whole. He added that their role had been essential in setting up national salary scales and that the need to work through the new Burnham Committee structures had had a consolidating effect.[29]

Indeed the setting up of the Burnham Committee was largely due to the AEC. Before the establishment of the committee each LEA had had its own local salary arrangements and there had been a great deal of variation between different authorities. In general terms teachers' pay had fallen badly behind in the inflation of the war years and by 1918 a very difficult situation had arisen with strikes in different parts of the country and with schools closed for quite long periods in some areas. The post-war demand for more teachers which the provisions of the Education Act of 1918 encouraged had the immediate effect of strengthening the bargaining position of the teachers, especially in the cities where they were most strongly unionised. The pressure was less strongly felt by local authorities in some of the county areas. Before the end of the war Fisher appointed two departmental committees 'to inquire into the principles' which should determine teachers' salary scales in elementary and in secondary schools. The report from the elementary committee did not recommend a single national scale but it did put forward principles which should govern the salary scales in future.[30] The existing variations in salary payments were so large that no single scale appeared to be possible.

In the continuing unrest among teachers the pressure for national scales came largely from the education committees in urban areas. Early in 1919 representatives of the AEC met Selby-Bigge at the Board to press the need for unified pay scales as a way of resisting upward escalation of salaries in those places where teachers were most strongly organised and where the shortage of staff was most acutely felt.[31] In January the AMC, the CCA and the AEC had set up a joint committee to confer on the possibility of establishing a common scale of salaries throughout the country. Within the committee it proved impossible to obtain agreement since some, including the AEC representatives, wished to see urgent action while others felt the time inopportune. At its annual general meeting in June the AEC resolved that the introduction of a national scale of salaries for teachers was a matter of 'urgent necessity' and asked the Board of Education 'to summon a conference, at the earliest possible date, of representatives of associations concerned in the administration of education, and of the recognised teachers' organisations, with a view to the preparation of such a scale.'[32]

The AEC's pressure gave the President of the Board of Education the opportunity to push matters to a conclusion. Representatives of the Association saw Fisher on 4 July and in a letter dated 8 July to its chairman he stated that he now intended to establish an organisation representing teachers and local authorities to discuss and keep under review on a national basis the remuneration of teachers. Fisher added that although the Board was prepared to see the salaries of teachers in elementary schools dealt with first, the organisation would not be satisfactory unless it was competent to deal with matters affecting the whole body of teachers including those in secondary schools and technical institutions. Meetings between the teachers and the local authority organisations in late July and early August at the Board of Education produced an agreement to set up a standing joint committee composed of representatives of the local authorities and of the National Union of Teachers (NUT) to negotiate on minimum pay scales for teachers in elementary schools.[33] The membership of the standing committee amounted to 44 and included 22 representatives from the NUT on one side and on the other 8 representatives from the CCA, 6 from the AMC, 6 from the AEC and 2 from London County Council. The Chairman was to be Lord Burnham. A similar committee, but on the teachers' side representative of secondary teachers' associations, was set up for secondary schools. The establishment of this committee was delayed somewhat by the County Councils Association's attempt to make its agreement to the formation of the committee conditional upon larger government grants for secondary education. The CCA stood alone in its manoeuvre. The executive committee of the AEC went so far as to urge the President of the Board of Education to nominate other persons to fill the CCA's places on the proposed standing committee.[34]

The attitude of the teachers' associations towards national salary scales was not as unambiguous as might be expected in retrospect. While the secondary teachers' organisations welcomed the idea, the NUT was equivocal. An editorial article in its journal, *The Schoolmaster*, argued strongly against any national scale as late as May 1919.[35] The Union's more active local associations were in the cities where they had been able to obtain salaries for their members which were much higher than anything which rural authorities seemed likely to accept. Thus a national scale could weaken rather than assist the position of teachers in such places. It was in order to accommodate this situation that the salaries for teachers in elementary schools eventually took the form of four different scales applying in different places – the highest in the cities, the lowest in rural areas.

The influence of education committees on national policy in the second decade of this century was shown by the extent to which their representatives had some effect on the contents of the Education Act of 1918. Geoffrey Sherington has shown that this measure consisted in many ways of ideas and initiatives which the Board of Education had developed but had been unable to enact before the First World War began and that the war itself acted as a catalyst[36].

When the bill was first published in 1917 the AEC called a special

general meeting which expressed strong support for the main reforms proposed including the raising of the leaving age, avoidance of
broken school terms, introduction of compulsory attendance at continuation schools for young people who left school before the age of
eighteen, closer regulation of the employment of children and the
promotion of social and physical training. But the main purpose of
the special general meeting was to express the opposition of many
education committees to clauses which would have enabled the
Board to create provincial councils, to take away its powers from a
Part III authority and give them to the appropriate county authority
where this seemed appropriate and to transfer from the courts to the
Board of Education the right to determine any appeal from a local
authority concerning its powers under education legislation. The
meeting went rather further than opposing proposals made by the
Bill to strengthen – as the Board saw it – local educational
administration. It also resolved that no Education Bill would be
acceptable which failed to permit any Part III authority 'to secure
full powers of initiation and administration or complete autonomy in
matters of higher education under Part II of the [1902] Act . . . if it
is in a position to exercise such powers with advantage.'[37]

Fisher's proposals for educational reform received widespread
support but he deliberately avoided the central denominational issue
of the dual system in order not to stir conflict and opposition at a
difficult time in the war. His anxiety to avoid conflict over the Bill
led him to agree to withdraw the administrative provisions to which
many education committees objected. The report of the meeting of
an AEC deputation with the President stated that he 'intimated his
willingness to make alterations to meet the views of the deputation,
on the understanding that if such alterations were agreed opposition
to the second reading of the bill on the part of the Association would
be withdrawn. This was accepted by the deputation.'[38] On the other
hand the AEC made no progress with its proposal that Part III
education authorities should be able to take Part II powers. The
Board made it clear that there was no possibility of making progress
with this proposal since it would certainly incur the strongest
opposition from the county councils.

According to Selby-Bigge the main theme of the Act of 1918 was
that of 'systematization' – the adequate contribution in every area by
every LEA to a national system of education accessible on the basis
of equal opportunity to every person capable of benefiting from it.
The changes in the Bill which the AEC successfully pressed for

presumably weakened the extent to which national systematization proved to be possible. The criticism of the system of administration between the wars made by civil servants preparing the Act of 1944 was that it reduced the Board of Education to a reactive agency – it could only ever react to initiatives from the local authorities and lacked either the power or the authority needed to give leadership at the national level. Writing soon after the legislation of 1918 and of its essential re-enactment in 1921, Selby-Bigge claimed that the Act embodied a new conception of the relation of central and local authorities. 'While the duty of securing its "adequacy" as a contribution to a national service . . . remains with the central authority, the initiative for its construction is assigned to the local authority.' There was to be an 'active and constructive partnership', 'a joint enterprise with reciprocal duties and responsibilities for the national interest'.[39] This is not the place to attempt to analyse the reasons for the great inequalities of educational provision between different authorities which became apparent to the wider public after the evacuation of schools and pupils in 1939, but a system in which some LEAs had wider responsibilities than others was bound to make it more difficult for authorities to work together and to move forward to the extent that was achieved after 1944. The unsatisfactory nature of the Part II and Part III division was apparent to the Board in 1918 but – as with the denominational difficulties – it was not possible for political reasons to move away from the position established by the Act of 1902.

It was not until after the reorganisation of local education authority administration in 1945, following the abolition of separate authorities for elementary education in many districts, that it really became possible for one organisation to represent the interests of all education committees. But immediately after the First World War the AEC tried to draw all committees together. In 1919 the Executive approved a draft letter proposed by the Secretary to be sent to all county education committees inviting them to join the Association. The membership then amounted to 238 committees, namely:

county boroughs	78
non-county boroughs	115
urban districts	45
	238

Since there were 251 education committees in the towns, there remained thirteen which were not in membership. These were said to be nearly all of comparatively small districts.[40] A number of county committees did join the Association during the next few years including Middlesex,

Flintshire, Wiltshire, East Suffolk, Hampshire, Hereford, Northumberland and Rutland but many remained outside. The differences between Part II and Part III authorities also made themselves felt at times within the Association. Some representatives from Part III authorities raised the matter of their representation on the executive committee at the annual general meeting in 1920. The basis of the complaint was that while there were 164 Part III authorities in membership they had only nine seats on the executive committee while the eighty-nine Part II authorities had a total of twenty seats.

Until 1919 all the annual meetings of the AEC were held in London, but there was no office there. The everyday business and correspondence of the Association was conducted from the work place of the incumbent honorary secretary or treasurer. The absence of a permanent headquarters and of a full-time secretariat has doubtless contributed to the lack of surviving records for the first part of the century. It also seems to have had the effect of denying the Association at the time the standing or status that it might have expected. In 1925 Percival Sharp, director of education for Sheffield, became honorary secretary – the fifth person since 1904 to hold that office. By the mid-1920s the growth of the AEC's influence can be seen in the large and varied list of public bodies and committees to which it nominated representatives. Apart from the Burnham committees, it was also represented on three ministerial committees, the Secondary Schools Examinations Council, the National Committee on Adult Education, City and Guilds of London Institute, National Institute for the Blind and the National Committee on Broadcasting.[41] Sharp saw the need for a permanent office and the ways of achieving this received a good deal of consideration in the years immediately following his appointment.

A sub-committee reported in 1927 that finances did not permit the establishment of an office 'on a scale commensurate with the importance of the work which it is desirable should be done'. When enough money was available it recommended that a permanent office be opened in London under the control of a full time chief officer with an efficient staff. The headquarters office should be associated with the management of the journal *Education* and the honorary secretary should be authorised to use its columns for issuing information of general interest.[42] It was only in 1932 that the AEC got its London office at 44 Russell Square where Sharp had a staff of four. Six years later the office moved to 10 Queen Anne Street where it was to remain apart from temporary removal for wartime evacuation.

The Association had acquired its own journal, *Education*, as a result of an agreement made in 1924. Negotiations with a Mr Hyams who was editor and chief proprietor of *Education* led to the AEC buying the company, keeping Hyams as editor and manager for five years at a fixed salary of £600 a year with bonuses payable in various circumstances. The arrangements were negotiated by Sharp and the final tranche of shares in the company – Councils and Education Press – was purchased before the end of 1925.[43]

Inter-war economies

During the years between the wars the prevailing political climate for most of the time gave a low priority to education. Education committees too often found themselves battling to sustain what they had already established rather than undertaking any new developments, however desirable. The first major attack came in 1922 in the form of the report of the Geddes Committee on economies which proposed such outrageous cuts in education that Fisher threatened to resign from office. Opposition generally was strong, two by-elections were lost by the government and the massive cuts were averted but free places to secondary schools and maintenance allowances were restricted and the new state scholarships to universities abandoned. The return of the Labour government to office in 1924 reversed those measures.

The election of the Baldwin government led to a further squeeze on educational expenditure. In 1925 the Board of Education proposed to reduce permitted expenditure by local authorities and then to freeze it at the reduced level for the next three years. LEAs mounted a strong campaign against these proposals which would have destroyed the percentage grant system on which the Burnham arrangements and, indeed, all other educational provision rested. While the different local authority associations worked together in opposing this attempt by the Board to reduce and freeze their educational expenditure, it should perhaps be noted that the direction of their complaints varied in a characteristic manner. The AEC called for the withdrawal of Circular 1371 which embodied the proposed policy, sought discussions with Lord Percy, President of the Board, to consider ways of improving the percentage grant systems and stressed the need to maintain educational expenditure. The County Councils Association joined in protesting against the new policy but the immediate thrust of its complaint was rather different for it resolved to protest 'against the action of the Board of Education in making, in advance of such revision, a rule compelling local education authorities generally to pay to their teachers the scales of the Burnham Award.'[44] In spite of attacks on the percentage grant system in the name of economy, it was maintained and after the Second World War secondary school costs came to be included within a modified formula. It was finally abolished in 1958 in rather different circumstances.

Towards the single, all purpose, education authority

The issue of the possible reform of local administration itself was never far from the minds of administrators and politicians in the later 1920s and the 1930s. The major Local Government Act of 1929 was not intended to make any change in the pattern of local educational administration but it did have the effect of creating some new local authorities which were large enough to adopt Part III status for elementary education. The county councils were most anxious to prevent this from happening and a brief agreed Bill was introduced by Trevelyan, Labour President of the Board of Education, in 1930 after discussion and agreement with Percy and Chamberlain of the Opposition to disqualify the new authorities from claiming Part III status.[45]

The political situation and the low priority accorded to education by successive governments during the inter-war years really meant that much of the Education Act of 1918 remained unfulfilled and that the Second World War was to prove the occasion for completing many of the reforms which had been stalled earlier. If the 1930s were dominated by economies in the public sector coupled with some priority for re-armament in later years, then the war years in a political sense produced the reaction against this neglect of services such as education. Indeed, as the war made ever deeper inroads into the lives of individuals, so did the pressures in society for the reform, improvement and extension of the educational system increase. Education committees found that the systems for which they were responsible came under much closer public scrutiny and criticism. Many of the issues to which the officials of the Board of Education turned in considering the future pattern of the nation's education service were matters which the office had been writing papers on and considering internally for many years. Two particularly difficult issues about which more had been written yet less accomplished than any others were both the products of the political realities behind the 1902 Act: the dual system and the system of having two types of education authority, one with much wider powers than the other. Butler was later to say that if Fisher had dealt with these issues in 1918, the 1944 Act would have been unnecessary. Many paragraphs in a paper on the position of the Part II and Part III authorities which RN Heaton produced for ministers in 1943 were in fact copied word for word from a paper produced for their predecessors in 1913.[46]

This issue had never been quiescent for any length of time since 1902 and the inquiry into devolution from the larger county authorities in the years before the First World War. Apart from becoming a matter of some public controversy again at the time of the Fisher Act, it tended also to obtrude when more purely educational matters were under consideration as in the deliberations of the Consultative Committee under the chairmanship of Sir Henry Hadow in 1925 and 1926. When the committee reported it felt obliged to treat of this issue since the traditional division between elementary and secondary codes of regulation meant that any recommendations for the post-primary education of all adolescents over the age of eleven were bound to be dealt with in a piecemeal fashion by the separate authorities for elementary and secondary schooling where Part III authorities existed. The committee reported the comment of one county education officer that in his county there were thirteen Part III authorities resulting in a situation where the education of that county had to be fitted into thirteen systems, 'a task that almost passed the wit of man'. At the same time the committee found that in many places relations between the two layers of authorities were 'tolerably friendly'. The committee regarded central schools and classes, senior schools, senior departments and 'higher tops' for children over eleven as belonging properly to the secondary stage of education yet they were provided by elementary education authorities.

> Will it be possible in the future for the country to acquiesce permanently in the division of part of the secondary grade of education between two separate authorities in the same area, with the result that an authority for

elementary education only may start a modern school or senior class when neighbouring 'secondary' schools under the administration of the authority for higher education are not fully used.[47]

Outside of the world of education, the May Committee on National Expenditure (1931) and the Select Committee on the Estimates (1939) both looked to the introduction of a single type of all-purpose education authority.

The Board of Education's Green Book *Education after the War* (1941), which contained most of the proposals that went into the Education Act of 1944, outlined the issues but did not recommend any particular solution. One member of the War Cabinet, Arthur Greenwood, had formal responsibility for post-war reconstruction in general terms and he had asked the Solicitor-General, Sir William Jowitt, to undertake a study of the future shape of local government with special reference to contemporary theories concerning regionalism. Thus at the time that the Green Book was being prepared, the permanent secretary, Holmes, was sending two papers on local education authorities to the Ministry of Health for the Solicitor-General. The first of these set out the existing position and explained that the creation of two types of authority was the outcome of political expediency rather than of any suitability to the educational system. The period since 1902 had demonstrated fully 'that this artificial dichotomy is a serious bar to educational progress'. There was no prospect of any reform arising out of local action since 'the full force of vested interests will be marshalled in support of the maintenance of the status quo'. The new element if the Green Book's proposals were accepted would be that all schools for pupils over eleven would be regarded as secondary. The field of elementary education would then be limited to pupils under eleven. The suggestion that the functions of authorities for elementary education should be limited to children up to eleven 'is only made to be rejected'. The second paper made it clear that the ideal system would be for the Board of Education to be empowered to prepare its own 'selective schedule of new local education authorities' but this would be impracticable 'in the circumstances of existing Parliamentary procedure'. The simplest solution might be simply to suppress all Part III authorities and pass their powers and duties to the relevant county authority. The political difficulty involved, however, led to the conclusion that it might be best to draw a new datum-line of 50,000 population. This would enable thirty-four existing Part III authorities to join the existing Part II LEAs as all-purpose education authorities. From the Parliamentary point of view, this was thought to be the preferable alternative since it would reduce the number of existing areas aggrieved at losing their functions as Part III authorities.[48]

Following minor changes in the status of some local authorities since 1902 the current position in 1941 was that there were 315 LEAs, viz:

63 County Councils
83 County Borough Councils
147 Borough Councils ⎱ with powers over elementary
22 Urban District Councils ⎰ schooling only, i.e. Part III

On publication of the Green Book in 1941, every educational body, as well as churches and political parties, put forward their post-war plans or hopes for educational reform. Those of the local authority associations included reactions to this administrative issue. The views were predictable. The Association of Municipal Corporations strongly opposed any regional organisation which might have limited the powers of their county borough members. It agreed that one type of education authority was desirable but no action should be taken to abolish or reduce the number of Part III authorities. It recommended a full and impartial inquiry before any action was taken. The County Councils Association saw no reason to dissent from the view that there should be a single type of education authority. The Federation of Part III Authorities resolved that in 'the interests of educational progress' they should not suffer any diminution in status.[49]

At this time the AEC represented all county boroughs, all but one of the Part III authorities but only a minority of counties (twenty-five out of sixty-three). By its efforts between the wars it had been slowly building up its membership among the county education committees although fewer than half had so far joined. It would clearly have some difficulty in speaking on this issue with unanimity. It could really only pursue the policy of suggesting no change until the general structure of local government had been reviewed. In its full report on the Green Book it stated that it could not agree that large numbers of authorities should disappear before 'adequate enquiry and report had been made'.[50]

In the Board of Education it was clear that local authority opposition might be easier to overcome if there could be a committee of inquiry and a report making clear the need to reform the Part II/Part

III arrangement. But it was thought to be very difficult to assemble a suitable committee of inquiry in wartime and the delay which this would involve might well lead to the loss of any suitable opportunity to introduce a general measure of educational reform. The Lord President's Committee of the Cabinet decided against a committee and asked the Paymaster-General to look into the matter and advise. It might perhaps be worth quoting from Butler's minute to the permanent secretary after this meeting for the flavour it gives of the President's views

> . . . I now suggest that LEAs be informed that no less a man than the Minister of Reconstruction [also held by Jowitt, the Paymaster General] will hear their plaints and receive their submissions with a view to reporting to me when he has been able to form a judgment. I have no doubt that the Parliamentary Secretary [Chuter Ede] would aid Sir Wm Jowitt, but since he is one of us, his name should be kept back.
> If you agree, would you try a draft to the authorities which should attempt in silky tones to make the most of this device?[51]

While the sequence of events moved forward in the intended manner, an incursion from the Ministry of Health had to be dealt with. It was proposing to constitute the new post-war health authorities to cover much larger areas than counties on the grounds that larger areas were needed for the economic provision of hospital facilities, that many counties and county boroughs were financially weak and that the medical profession had made very clear that it was unwilling to serve under the existing local authorities. In order to avoid a lack of public interest and very low polls in elections to these large authorities, the Ministry proposed that education, highways, planning, police and the fire service should also become their responsibility. The Board strongly opposed these proposals, believing that such very large units would be quite inappropriate and much too remote for the administration of schools and colleges.[52]

During the winter of 1942–43 Chuter Ede gave attention to this problem and it was he who suggested the eventual solution. From the AEC, Sharp had increasingly taken the line that difficulties could be overcome through more cooperation. In a minute to Chuter Ede, Heaton reported on the attitudes of the various associations and commented that, 'although cooperation was one of the most hallowed words in the educational vocabulary, when it came to deeds, the ship of cooperation foundered on the rocks of local jealousies and civic self-importance'. Ede took up this point in a minute to Butler, commenting that a very successful delaying action had been fought by the Part III authorities under that banner, 'but if their object was to achieve cooperation they must feel that their history for self-preservation has not brought them much nearer this desirable manifestation of life in the educational world'. He went on to argue that the present bulk of Part III authorities did not govern areas which would give a sufficient population for a well-balanced secondary school system. At the same time the disadvantage of county government was that its administration was too remote.

> It is for these reasons that I have thought that an adaptation of the Guardians' Committees established under the Local Government Act, 1929, is the appropriate form in which the detailed local administration of education should be cast. On the assumption that only counties and county boroughs were education authorities, 'I would ensure that where a county district had 7,000 children it should have the right to a district committee.'[53]

Jowitt received the representations of the local authority associations and from some individual authorities as well as papers from the Board of Education. It was not, perhaps, surprising that his recommendations were in line with the Board's thinking. Counties and county boroughs alone should be LEAs. Counties should be given wide powers to delegate if they wished. Failing an agreed scheme primary and secondary education in Part III areas with more than 7,000 pupils should be referred to joint committees with half the members from the county and half from the district council with a county appointed chairman. In Chuter Ede's ideas (which were of course reflected in this report) lay the principal features of the 1944 settlement of this issue. The Part III authorities were to go, but the larger would have the right to their own divisional executive, to be known as excepted districts while county authorities could, if they wished, set up other divisional executives for smaller districts or for combinations of districts. But since neither of these bodies were to be education authorities, they could raise no rate and were entirely incorporated in their counties. In the words of the 1943 white paper, they were to be 'entrusted with the general duty of keeping the educational needs of the area under review and making recommendations to the county education committee.'[54]

At this time Percival Sharp was very ill and he was absent from the executive committee of the AEC when it debated the white paper's proposals on 19 and 20 August. As might have been expected, the differences between county and Part III authority members showed through. After discussion in which the general tone was hostile to the proposals and supportive of efforts to save the Part III authorities, the president, Cropper (Chesterfield), Innes (Birmingham) and either Aitken or Meadon (both Lancashire) were asked to draft suitable resolutions, but Aitken and Meadon as representatives of the county interest declined to cooperate.[55] Nevertheless resolutions in defence of the Part III position were adopted by the executive committee. The small authorities were a majority at the forthcoming conference and inevitably the resolutions had to appeal to them. Whatever might have been said at this stage, there was really no longer any possibility of Part III authorities being given powers in the forthcoming legislation.

When the first schedule of the Education Bill which dealt with this question was taken in the Commons, members from towns which were not to be recognised as education authorities argued the case for their urban districts and non-county boroughs vigorously, as in 1902. But Butler felt he could make no concessions beyond the provision for divisional executives and excepted districts and he gained the support of the Lord President's Home Affairs Committee of the Cabinet for this view.[56] He himself wrote much later that since this debate came after the revolt of the Commons on the equal pay issue and the reversal of that vote by a vote of confidence at the behest of the Prime Minister, 'thereafter no members proved to be so bold as to press an amendment which was unacceptable to the government if there was any prospect of it being carried. This made it very much easier to deal with the potentially controversial abolition of the Part III authorities.'[57]

References

1 PRO. ED. 24/126, Memorandum, 'Clause 26 of the Education Bill 1906'.
2 *Parliamentary Debates* (Fourth Series) Vol. CVII col. 658, (5 May 1902).
3 PRO. ED. 24/126, Henry Hobhouse (CCA) to Birrell (President of Board of Education), 3 May 1906.
4 *Ibid.*, Morant to Hobhouse, 4 July 1906.
5 AEC, Executive Committee Minutes, 14 Mar. 1906 and 24 Apr. 1906.

6   AEC, AGM, Resolutions affecting the New Education Bill (1906), 14 and 15 June 1906.

7   PRO. ED. 24/120, History of the Education Bill 1906, C. Eaton, Jan. 1907.

8   AHD Acland had been Liberal MP for Rotherham and held office as Vice-President of the Committee of Council for Education during Gladstone's fourth ministry (1892–5). After the 1902 Act he was chairman of the West Riding Higher Education Sub-Committee.

9   Board of Education, *Report of the Consultative Committee upon the question of devolution by county education authorities*, Cd. 3952, 1908.

10 *School Government Chronicle*, 8 Oct. 1904, p. 353.

11 AEC, *Annual Report for 1904–1905*, 1905. p. 4.

12 *School Government Chronicle*, 8 June 1907, p. 513.

13 PRO. ED. 24/14, 'Points against *Ad Hoc*' by RL Morant.

14 *School Government Chronicle*, 3 June, 1911, pp. 514–5; p. 501.

15 AEC, Executive Committee Minutes, 20 Oct. 1911.

16 *Ibid.* Memo Proposed Council of Education for England attached to Minutes dated 24 Jan. 1912.

17 *Ibid.*, T Groves, (Hon. Secy. AEC) to CH Wyatt (Manchester), 24 Jan. 1912.

18 PRO. ED. 24/1385, Selby-Bigge to Pease, 9 Dec. 1911.

19 *Ibid.*, Selby-Bigge to Pease, 12 Feb. 1912.

20 *Ibid.*, Selby-Bigge to Pease, 11 July 1912.

21 AEC, Executive Committee Minutes, 27 Nov. 1912 and 16 Jan. 1913.

22 PRO. ED. 24/1385, Selby-Bigge to Pease, 11 July 1912.

23 *School Government Chroncile*, 7 June 1913, p. 493 et. seq.

24 PRO. ED. 24/629, 'Necessity for increased financial aid for local education authorities in 1914–1915', 13 Dec. 1913.

25 Treasury, Departmental Committee on Local Taxation, *Final Report*, (Cd. 7315), 1914, p. 100.

26 *School Government Chronicle*, 13 June 1914, p. 549.

27 Geoffrey Sherington, *English Education, Social Change and War 1911–20*, 1981, pp. 45–8.

28 *School Government Chronicle*, 5 June 1915, p. 375; *Ibid.*, 16 June, 1917, p. 292.

29 LA Selby-Bigge, *The Board of Education*, 1927, pp. 194–5.

30 Board of Education, *Report of the Departmental Committee for inquiring into the principles which should determine the construction of scales of salary for teachers in elementary-schools*, Cd. 8939, 1918.

31 PRO. ED. 108/23, Notes of an interview between the secretary of the Board and representatives of the AEC, 14 March 1919.

32 AEC, Annual General Meeting, Minutes, 5 June 1919.

33 AEC, Executive Committee Minutes, 25 July 1919; Letter HAL Fisher to President of AEC, 8 July 1919 and Minutes: PRO. ED. 108/23, Resolutions passed at a meeting of the Constituent Committee, 12 Aug. 1919.

34 AEC, Executive Committee Minutes, 6 Feb. 1920.

35 *The Schoolmaster*, 24 May 1919, p. 807.

36 G Sherington, *op. cit.*, p. 117.

37   AEC, Minutes of a Special General Meeting, 30 Oct. 1917.

38   AEC, Executive Committee Minutes, 20 Nov. 1917.

39   LA Selby-Bigge, *op. cit.*, p. 187.

40   AEC, Executive Committee Minutes, 24 April 1919; Minutes of the AGM, 5 June 1919.

41   AEC, Executive Committee Minutes, 8 July 1927.

42   *Ibid.*, 24 Sept. 1927.

43   *Ibid.*, 2 May 1924 and 15 Oct. 1925.

44   Board of Education, Circular 1371, 25 Nov. 1925: AEC, Executive Committee Minutes, 4 Dec. 1925 and 11 Mar. 1926; Correspondence P Sharp to education committees, 21 Dec. 1925 [in Minute Book].

45   PRO. ED. 24/1151, Note on Education (Local Authorities) Bill, 1930.

46   PRO., ED 24/2078, Local Education Areas. Distinction between Part II and Part III, H.W.O., 28 Jan. 1913 and ED 136/357, The Units of LEA Administration, Apr. 1943.

47   Board of Education, *Education of the Adolescent*, Report of the Consultative Committee, 1926, pp. 163–4.

48   PRO., ED 136/301, M G Holmes to J Maude (Ministry of Health), 6 May 1941.

49   PRO., ED 136/236, AMC, Report adopted 23 July 1942, paras 43–5; ED 136/251, CCA, Draft Report of the Education Advisory Sub-Committee, p. 10, 29 Nov. 1941; ED 136/255, Federation of Part III Education Committees, Statement of Policy adopted 10 June 1942.

50   PRO., ED 136/215, Note of discussion with committee of AEC by Holmes, 25 July 1941; AEC, Report of Special Sub-Committee on *Education after the War*, 1942.

51   PRO., ED 136/351, R A Butler to Secretary, 6 July 1942.

52   PRO., ED 136/358, Bosworth-Smith to Holmes, 1 Feb. 1943; ED 136/359, Maude to Alexander Maxwell, 19 Apr. 1943; Holmes to Butler, 1 May 1943.

53   PRO., ED 136/351, J C E[de] to Secretary and President, 11 Feb. 1943; Jowitt to Butler, 19 Feb. 1943; ED 136/357, J C E[de] to President, 14 Apr. 1943.

54   Board of Education, *Educational Reconstruction*, Cmnd. 6458, 1943, paras 117–8.

55   PRO., ED 136/356, Personal notes on a recent meeting of the AEC Executive, R Beloe to Chuter Ede, n.d.

56   PRO., ED 136/525, War Cabinet, Lord President's Committee, LP (44) 74, 26 Apr. 1944.

57   Lord Butler, *The Art of the Possible*, 1971, p. 122.

Chapter 3

The influence of education committees in the years following the Butler Act

The situation

While there were extensive consultations with local authority associations over the possible content of the Education Act of 1944, it would be wrong to give the impression that these had a decisive effect on the main provisions of that measure. The spirit that lay behind the Act, both in the popular mind and in the minds of those who drafted it, was asserted in Section 1

> 'It shall be the duty of the Minister of Education to promote the education of the people of England and Wales and the progressive development of institutions devoted to that purpose, and to secure the effective execution by local authorities, under his control and direction, of national policy for providing a comprehensive educational service in every area'.

In initiating discussions among the most senior officials within the Board, the Permanent Secretary, Maurice Holmes, sounded this note when he invited them to the first meeting in his room explaining that 'other persons and bodies have ideas on post-war educational reconstruction, and I think this is a matter in which the Board should lead rather than follow. . . .'[1]

In replying to this, the Deputy Secretary, Richard Wood, was more specific. The balance of power had passed to the LEAs and the Board came to leave the field to others. This had been due in no small measure to the attitude of Lord Percy who, as President (1924–29) had belittled 'the powers and position of the department' . . . 'I do not think we have ever recovered from the damage of that period, but the prospect of educational reconstruction that lies ahead offers an admirable opportunity for re-establishing the position of the Board as the body competent to lead and to direct the educational system of the country'. Wood also favoured more regular consultation with directors of education and teachers. Sir Percival Sharp and his association had come to occupy an unjustifiably privileged position.[2] The stress laid on the need for the Board to assert its position of leadership reflected public feeling that greater centralization and more emphasis on national policy was essential to undo the inequity and inadequacy of educational provision in many districts and unevenness between authorities which became apparent with wartime evacuation and population movement. Thus the initiative over educational reconstruction remained very much with the Board.

The evidence of the Board's papers show that at different times it turned for confidential advice to A L Binns, then chief education officer of the West Riding and Chairman of the Association of Directors and Secretaries for Education, while the Parliamentary Secretary, Chuter Ede, seems to have obtained private advice from R Beloe, county education officer for Surrey. Percival Sharp did not enjoy the same measure of confidence among the Board's officials as Alexander later came to enjoy. Sharp's own record of service in the government of education was outstanding. From the end of the First World War until his retirement in 1932 at the age of sixty-five he was director of education for Sheffield. He became part-time secretary of the AEC in 1925 and was full-time secretary from 1932 to 1944. He had been a member of the executive of the association since 1911 and was influential in establishing the Burnham Committee of which he was a member from 1919 to 1949 and secretary of the local authorities panel from 1925 to 1945. He had come to teaching through the pupil-teacher system and taught mathematics and science. Lord Percy was later to write of Sharp as the AEC's 'Chief professional henchman' and also described him as 'a little combative bull-terrier of a man, a supremely able organiser who had, however, come to the top the hard way and seemed to me to look at education always rather from the extinct pupil-teacher's point of view'. From 1937 Sharp contributed a column entitled 'Week by Week' to *Education* in which he wrote of issues of current interest to educational administrators and others – a practice continued by his successor. Comments in the Board's files illustrate the annoyance this column caused on occasion to some civil servants. At the time of the Spens Report in 1938 Holmes minuted the comment that 'Experience shows that however much one might impress on him (Sharp) that such and such a piece of information is strictly confidential, he invariably publishes it, or its substance, in the next issue of *Education*'.[4] Butler and Holmes both felt some difficulty in discussing their plans for the future of the dual system frankly with Sharp since they feared he would, by publicising their intentions prematurely, set one or other of the churches against them.[5]

The Act of 1944 spelt out more decisively than had previously been the case that it was the function of the central government to determine the nation's education policies and it was the duty of LEAs to provide services in their areas in accordance with statutory requirements. Yet, in the event, education committees acting together were to become more influential and, in important instances, initiated and pushed through national policies towards which the government of the day was indifferent or even initially hostile. The means by which they came to exercise such influence at the national level in the quarter century following the Butler Act was through a reconstructed AEC.

Sharp had really been in an impossible position in the discussions on the abolition of the Part III authorities and the reorganisation of local education administration. The apparent conflict of interests between county and Part III education committees has already been discussed. The future of the AEC itself was brought into question by the reorganisation. The revenue from subscriptions from member committees would fall from £2,850 to £1,200 p.a. since most of the subscription income was paid by Part III authorities. Only thirty-two county committees were in membership in January 1944. In correspondence with Butler, Alderman Cropper of Chesterfield, president of the AEC, explained that the association was considering admitting the new divisional executives and excepted districts to membership, but feared that counties which were not themselves members would refuse to pay the dues of any of their divisional bodies which might wish to join. Butler returned a bland and neutral reply.[6] Thus a reconstruction of the AEC itself was essential if it were to continue. At the same time the opportunities open to the Association if it were successfully recast would be greater than before since all education authorities would in future be all-purpose, there would not be two categories of authority whose interests appeared at times to be naturally poised for conflict on particular issues. Percival Sharp's retirement for health reasons at the end of 1944 led to the task of reconstruction falling on his successor, Dr William Alexander, who also moved from the position of director of education for Sheffield and became secretary of the AEC in January 1945.

William Alexander brought with him diverse experience of the education service. He had taught at both school and university level, had served as deputy director of education in Walthamstow and as director at Margate, a Part III authority. One of the earliest developments of his secretaryship of the AEC was a vigorous drive to replace the disappearing 169 Part III authorities in membership by county education committees which were still outside. Aided by a recommendation from the County Councils Association, – in which Sir Samuel Gurney-Dixon of Hampshire was influential – all county education committees joined the AEC. The Scottish education committees with their different system remained outside the Association but membership did extend to Northern Ireland and the accession of Londonderry Education Committee in 1955 marked the culmination of a maximum stable membership which was to be maintained until the difficulties of the 1970s led to the demise of the Association. It should, perhaps, be noted that the new divisional executives for education never joined since they did not have the powers of education committees and were not LEAs but they did form their own National Association of Divisional Executives for Education.

The achievement of unified representation of education committees led to a widening and deepening of the influence of committees at the national level through their organisation. One quantitative form of measurement of the standing of an organisation might be the extent to which it is offered representation on other bodies. The AEC was represented on sixty-three other bodies in 1947, seventy-eight ten years later and reached its highest level of ninety-seven by the time of local government reorganisation in 1973–4. These included examination boards, the Sports Council, the Field Studies Council, broadcasting organisations and various international bodies quite apart from such official committees as Burnham. It was in the immediate post-war years that the AEC matured into the 'single effective voice' for the maintained education system which it had always sought to be.

Thus education committees as a group through their Association, were most effective in their influence on national policy in the twenty years or so following the Butler Act. So widespread was their influence during that period that to examine it would almost be to write the history of the education system and that is not possible within the scope of this study. But as illustrations of the contribution of the committees and of the AEC to national policy generally the provision of schools and school building and the development of examinations and the curriculum will be examined.

School building

By 1945 successive governments had been dithering for twenty years over raising the minimum school leaving age from fourteen to fifteen. The strength of public opinion on this issue during the war had been such that the Coalition government had given an under-taking that the leaving age would be raised to fifteen no later than 1 April 1947. An additional year group in the schools would require about 400,000 more places and a considerable number of additional teachers. Standardised prefabricated classroom units which could be erected in playgrounds were developed to meet the situation and all appeared to be on course for the achievement of the target in spite of all sorts of immediate post-war difficulties and shortages – indeed the Minister of Education even described the decision to accommo-date the extra year group by 1947 as 'an act of faith rather than an act of wisdom'. Faced with severe financial and economic problems, the Treasury, working through a Cabinet committee, tried in January 1947 to achieve a last minute postponement of the appointed date. 'Rumour' of what was afoot reached the AEC. A special meeting of the executive was called for 16 January and a telegram sent to the Prime Minister urging the government to keep its pledge. The Cabinet met at 9 pm. that evening to consider the recommendations of its committee on economic planning one of these being to post-pone the raising of the leaving age. In the event the decision was finely balanced but enough of a stir had been created for a majority of those present at the Cabinet meeting to fear the political con-sequences of a postponement more than they feared the economic cost of implementation. In the words of the Cabinet record 'it was felt that the political disadvantage of breaking the pledges which had been given to Parliament outbalanced the economic benefits which would be derived from the proposal'.[7] The close involvement of the AEC in fending off this particular attempt to derail the much desired programme of educational reform was indicative of the way in which the Association came to operate from 1945 – alert to exploit every opportunity to press the case for education within the machinery of government. The Association rightly regarded this decision as the key to the State's attitude to all reforms for if it had gone the other way then the 1944 Act would itself have followed the 1918 Act into ineffectiveness.

Given the commitment of the achievement of the main aims of the Butler Act, the burden falling upon LEAs in providing schools and teachers was bound to be extremely heavy. Demography made the situation more difficult as the number of live births increased. Quite apart from providing a place in a secondary school for every boy and girl over the age of eleven instead of only one place for every seven in the age group as pre-war, the most urgent need for most of the time was to provide sufficient places for the growing total age groups. Table 3.1 gives some indication of the overall size of the problem.

Table 3.1 Pupils in maintained schools

Year	No. of pupils	Year	No. of pupils
1947	5,034,275	1963	6,925, 328
1951	5,737,698	1967	7,328,110
1955	6,515,676	1971	8,165,472
1959	6,901,187	1975	8,923,975

The growth in the number of live births during the war and the years immediately following meant that from the late 1940s the principal strategy had perforce to be that of providing sufficient new places for these larger age groups as they grew up through the system and using the opportunity to reorganise the provision for senior pupils into secondary schools. When the Butler Act was passed, the task of providing a secondary school place for every pupil over the age of eleven was thought to be so great that there were fears among officials in the Board of Education that this principal reform might not be achieved in practice for an indefinite period. That the much more difficult situation of putting the reform into practice and providing places by the mid-1960s for rather more than a million additional children was successfully handled was really due to the development of a close working relationship between the Ministry and the local authorities.

Not since the decade following the Education Act of 1870 had so many new school places been built within comparatively few years as were to be provided in the years following the Second World War. The existing procedures had served such school building as had been required before the War, but the 1920s and 1930s were not a period marked by the building of schools, the required sequence of pre-liminaries for the choice and provision of sites had been considered rather more leisurely in pre-war circumstances. It was likely to prove quite impractical in the new situation. Thus the issue of choosing and buying sites was one of the earliest and potentially most vexing problems which confronted LEAs as they set about their task of providing schools. The matter was further complicated by the failure of central government to make adequate allowance for inflation of land values since under the Town and Country Planning Act it was only feasible to pay the 1939 value plus 30 per cent. Even when the vendor was willing to sell voluntarily on this basis, the full acquisition process including the obtaining of planning permission, Ministry of Education agreement to the site and actual purchase was found to take up to a year. The price offered meant that often resort had to be made to a compulsory purchase order.[8]

The problems which would arise from all this were being dis-cussed within the Ministry and with the AEC early in 1946. It was accepted in the Ministry that the amount of building which lay ahead was so great that not only must speedy methods of construction be used but the preliminary planning and administrative procedures would have to be simplified and expedited. By the end of April the decision had been taken to set up a committee to 'look at school sites and building procedures'. When Burrows and Jackman of the Ministry first spoke to Alexander it was understood that the arrangement would be an informal one of people likely to know the machinery, but not representative of all the various associations and the latter suggested that the LEA side should consist of himself, Barraclough (North Riding), Stillman (Middlesex County Architect) and Rothwell (Sheffield City Estates Surveyor and presumably known to Alexander from his Sheffield days). On the Ministry side there were to be five members. At the beginning of May, Alexander accepted a written invitation from Burrows to join the 'informal committee'. Within a week the 'informal committee' had changed in the Ministry file to an established 'Sites and Building Committee'. The first meeting was held on 21 June with W C Cleary of the Ministry as Chairman.[9]

The report of the Committee was sent to LEAs with Circular 130 on 15 November 1946. The membership, officially appointed by the Minister, was as first discussed with Alexander except that Rothwell of Sheffield had been unable to take up the invitation and Woodhead (Kent County Education Officer) and Hayward (West Sussex County Clerk) were added. From the files there can be no doubt of the crucial influence of the AEC on the Sites and Building Committee and among the AEC members it might be noted that Frank Barraclough's advice in particular seems to have been generally accepted and may be found little changed in the Committee's report. It can be traced since he was unable to attend some meetings and then sent long and detailed letters of advice not to the committee secretary but to the AEC so that the points made might be pressed. They included proposals that it should be possible to reserve land for educational as well as for residential or industrial purposes, that the definition of immediacy for sites should go beyond the three year period suggested and that when LEAs authorised the purchase of sites they should at the same time authorise the use of compulsory purchase powers if necessary so as to save time. All of these became recommendations, the second was met by the substitution of a five year period for the existing three.[10]

Apart from sites the committee had to make practical recommendations to deal with the problems associated with building. The development plans then being submitted by LEAs in fulfilment of their obligations under the 1944 Act contained a vast amount of building which would take years to complete and would have to be phased in some way. Alexander pressed the view that the committee must find ways of ensuring that the approval procedures of LEAs and the Ministry kept in phase with the actual rate of building. It was necessary to agree a period in which the implementation of the building projects would be carried out. Alexander and Woodhead both urged the committee to postulate a fifteen year period with a total expenditure at then current prices of £1,000,000,000. The AEC also pressed for a considerably larger fraction of the country's building force to be engaged on educational building than had been the case hitherto. The report as agreed accepted all these points – the total of £1,000,000,000 with average annual expenditure of 'approximately £70,000,000 a year which at present costs is roughly double the programme in 1938'. The report went on to emphasise that 'before the war between 3 and 4 per cent of the country's aggregate building force was employed on school construction and we envisage at least doubling the school building labour force'.[11]

Achieving anything like the tempo proposed in the report and then sustaining it against economic vagaries and Treasury pressure required a great deal of effort. It is not too much to claim that while it was central government which provided the legislative framework needed for post-war educational advance, it was the emergence of an efficient organisation representing the education committees which provided much of the pressure to mount an adequate building programme. In the early years the prospect of actually constructing £70,000,000 worth new buildings every year was viewed with some scepticism inside the Ministry. The actual achievement in money terms over the fifteen years was quite near to £1,000,000,000 in all, but as has been pointed out elsewhere, there are two further factors to be taken into account in considering how far this ambitious target was achieved.[12] The first of these is obviously the inflation of building costs and it has been calculated that if the total sum spent in buildings in the fifteen years from 1946–47 is reduced to constant 1946 prices this would be £612,900,000. On the other hand from 1951 and after it proved possible to make considerable unit cost savings in building construction work. Thus the actual volume of building achieved was probably very close to the amount envisaged in the School Sites and Building Committee.

Possibly the most critical threat to the impetus of the school building drive was posed when Florence Horsbrugh was Minister. She took office in 1951 and was the only head of the education department not to be a member of the Cabinet since the Second World War. If it be the function of the Minister (or Secretary of State) to ensure that adequate resources are made available to sustain the service for which she is responsible, then Florence Horsbrugh hardly measured up to the job. Under pressure from the Treasury, the Minister removed projects amounting to £28,000,000 from the building programme for 1952/53 leaving a programme of £42,000,000.[13] The new restrictive policies had been indicated by a circular which led the AEC to set up a special sub-committee to monitor and react as the situation might require. The new restrictive programme made it look as though the achievement of genuine secondary education for all was likely to be even further off. A survey undertaken by the AEC at the end of 1952 showed that nearly a quarter of a million pupils over the age of eleven remained in all-age schools.

The Commons Select Committee on the Estimates reported on education in 1953. While the main function of the Committee was to see that good value was obtained and that public money was spent wisely and with due regard to economy, it felt obliged to complain that the government's target for new school places was inadequate and that at least 100,000 more should have been provided by the end of 1953. The building of schools was found to be lagging seriously behind the building of homes so that some LEAs had been obliged to hire temporary accommodation and to spend exceptionally heavily on the provision of transport.[14] Florence Horsbrugh's position did not imporve the next year and she also got into difficulties over attempts to increase the contributions from teachers towards their superannuation scheme. On 18 October 1954, David Eccles succeeded her as Minister.

The appointment of Eccles marked the beginning of a decade of educational building, not only new schools but also new building for technical and higher education. After the criticisms of the Select Committee and the difficulties for the government arising out of the cuts imposed on the educational building programme, Eccles was no doubt reasonably well placed to get a different message across in the Cabinet and to the Treasury. He began by encouraging the reorganisation of rural all-age schools. The new policy was set out in a circular at the end of 1954. The Minister proposed to add to the 1955–56 building programme as much work for the reorganisation of all-age schools and the creation of secondary school places in rural areas as could be effected. County LEAs were asked to inform the Ministry by 15 January 1955 of any projects which could be actually started by March 1956 and to show which all-age schools would be reorganised as a consequence.[15] When the next round of Treasury cuts came early in 1956, Eccles was successful in protecting the building programme. The appreciation which the AEC felt for the Minister's efforts and, indeed, the warmth of their feelings towards him was possibly indicated by the rather unusual procedure of sending a personal letter to David Eccles expressing appreciation of his efforts. Alexander wrote

This is the second time within a matter of months in which the education service, which up to then had borne perhaps more than its fair share of cuts and economies, has virtually escaped serious interference with its broad development. The Committee have asked me to express to you their very great appreciation of the efforts which must undoubtedly have been made to ensure that this result came about. They feel that it is in no small measure due to your personal efforts and, just as this Association has not been slow to criticise certain actions and policies which they thought not to be in the interests of the education service, so they hasten to express their thanks for the satisfactory decisions which have been made regarding the building programmes.[16]

In terms of ministers holding office, not only David Eccles, Minister from 1954 to 1957 and again from 1959 to 1962, but also Geoffrey Lloyd, 1957 to 1959, and Edward Boyle, 1962 to 1964, all gave significant and powerful support to the cause of school building and by the mid-1960s the Butler Act's principal aim of secondary education for all had, in effect, been achieved. The extent of school building in the two decades following the end of the Second World War may be seen from Table 3.2. Quite apart from the apparently endless discussion with and pressure from LEAs to maintain the impetus of the programme, close cooperation between the Ministry and LEAs was essential to reduce costs and, later, to help create building consortia.

The reorganisation of the Ministry's architects branch and its buildings and priority branch into a single architects and building branch in 1949 proved to be an essential preliminary to the improvement in the rate of school building and reduction in costs in the 1950s. LEAs were never likely to allow the Ministry to forget that it was they who provided the schools and they were certainly not prepared to see new schools built by the central government or to its order and then be obliged to take them over. But when money was none too plentiful it was impossible to justify the existing variations in building costs incurred for similar places even by neighbouring authorities. In 1947, for instance, Huddersfield and Wakefield were able to build primary places at a cost of £80 each, yet Leeds at the same time had a unit cost for primary places of £240. In order to achieve a more economical approach to building schools the Ministry's building regulations might need to be reviewed, but quite apart from that, standardisation, bulk ordering, economical planning by the designer and possibly some prefabrication would all be needed if those economies in unit costs were to be attained which would permit a school building programme of the size required – yet all of these were primarily the concern of individual local authorities. Careful negotiations with the AEC and with individual LEAs were required if full advantage were to be obtained from these various measures. A great deal of time and energy was put into achieving this end.

Table 3.2 Number of new schools completed and places provided, 1946–65.

Year	Primary		Secondary	
	Schools	Places	Schools	Places
1946		20,000		14,040
1947	7	22,320	3	62,165
1948	15	37,765	13	96,890
1949	97	68,720	21	50,610
1950	191	89,280	48	38,360
1951	288	120,230	65	38,565
1952	439	156,620	49	46,765
1953	384	177,740	116	84,495
1954	436	125,015	160	72,035
1955	284	115,650	147	96,470
1956	225	107,595	214	130,575
1957	278	117,855	300	162,570
1958	221	98,080	375	196,830
1959	217	86,810	273	159,265
1960	225	83,305	187	133,525
1961	258	91,035	152	112,580
1962	269	81,490	130	112,880
1963	308	102,340	174	127,015
1964	393	116,250	187	161,970
1965	375	113,985	176	132,325

By the late 1950s the idea of local authorities forming building consortia to achieve greater economies and better value became increasingly acceptable. Perhaps the best known of these was the first to be set up, CLASP, which had its origins in the Nottinghamshire authority. Commended by the Select Committee on the Estimates in 1961, it was given a good deal of publicity by the Ministry which sought to encourage other local authorities to form similar groups. In June 1961 it published *The Story of CLASP* as Building Bulletin 19. Derek Morrell, then assistant secretary and joint head of the architects and building branch indicated the degree to which the success of such an initiative depended on local authorities when he wrote to Alexander

I think the point which I am keenest to have taken by the customers [LEAs] is that here is evidence of partnership in development work between central and local government, and of the excellent results that can be obtained when both sides regard their contribution as complementary one to the other. At the centre we are perhaps better placed than authorities to undertake basic research and development – establishing principles and solving basic technical problems. But our work will not bear fruit unless it is built upon and continuously improved in the manner of CLASP by local authorities, who alone can integrate it with the whole process of design and production, and who can alone engage in continuous further development within the essential context of a large building programme.[17]

Before concluding this brief examination of investment in school building, it might be useful to compare the extent to which public resources were devoted to the National Health Service, housing and education in the twenty years or so after the war. Administratively they were rather differently organised. The National Health Service (which did not include the school health service) was really controlled by the central government, its local and regional committees were partly nominated by the government and they depended entirely on the government for their funding. Housing was a local government service aided and overseen by a central government ministry rather like education up to a point. But there was an essential difference in that committees dealing with housing were simply local council committees, consisting only of council members and having no national organisation of their own. While it is difficult to make any meaningful comparison of capital investment in these three areas – partly because of differences of definition – it is possible to make the broad comparison of the totals of public expenditure in these three areas. Table 3.3 may serve to illustrate the strength of education's position.[18]

Table 3.3 Public expenditure summary

A Total expenditure in £ million (UK) at current prices			
	1951	1961	1966
National Health Service	498	930	1395
Education	398	1013	1768
Housing	404	555	975
B Expressed as percentages of public expenditure in each case			
National Health Service	8.4	9.0	9.1
Education	6.8	9.8	11.5
Housing	6.9	5.4	6.4

The raising of the school leaving age, the rise in the population of school age (Table 3.1), and a secondary school place for all pupils over the age of eleven all required more resources. The political will to provide the resources may have been due to a public belief in the need for and value of more educational facilities. If so, clearly it was more effective than ever before.

Examinations, the curriculum and the Schools Council

In school building and gaining resources for education the interests of education committees and of the Ministry were very similar. In the matter of the pattern of examinations and control over the curriculum that was often not the position. In retrospect it may be seen that the principal influence in shaping the secondary school examination pattern as it has existed for the last quarter of a century, and through that the curriculum, was the LEA interest often acting through the AEC.[19] The position in 1945 was that a wartime committee with Sir Cyril Norwood as its chairman had reported in favour of abolishing all external examinations for secondary school pupils below the age of eighteen. In other words the School Certificate – then taken by grammar school pupils at sixteen – was to be abolished but there was to be an examination at eighteen designed for those seeking entry to higher education. When the Norwood Report was published in 1943 it met with strong opposition from many secondary school teachers, some employing bodies and parents. The Report had faithfully reflected the predominant views in the inspectorate. Martin Roseveare (senior chief inspector) and many of his colleagues sustained their opinions and influenced Ministry attitudes in the post-war years.

Thus in 1946 Ellen Wilkinson sent a draft circular to local authority and teachers' associations supporting the view that the needs of pupils could best be met by freeing them from external examinations until the age of seventeen or eighteen. Public examinations at 16+ were to be discontinued as soon as possible. Other evidence has indicated that the new Minister was anxious to exercise fully the powers apparently conferred on her by the 1944 Act. In this matter the draft stated that the Minister would not be justified in limiting her functions to those of a coordinator as hitherto. In future she would assume full responsibility for the direction of policy and arrangements for school examinations. LEAs feared that this meant the central government was intending to take control of the curriculum. In its comment on the draft circular the AEC made clear its belief that the substantial influence which the Secondary Schools Examinations Council exercised over the curriculum 'renders it undesirable that the Minister should assume responsibility for the direction of policy in regard to school examinations'. Several months of critical negotiations followed and the Minister made two significant concessions. The circular itself was changed to state that the Minister would assume 'full responsibility *with the assistance of a reconstituted SSEC* for the direction of policy and general arrangements in regard to school examinations.' Secondly the local authority representation on the SSEC was increased from five to eight members.[20] This was a considerable victory for the LEAs and especially for the AEC which had been the lead organisation in the negotiations. The LEA element within the SSEC became the driving force which established the General Certificate of Education (GCE) '0' and 'A' levels to replace the School Certificates and Higher School Certificates as the public examinations for grammar school pupils at sixteen and eighteen thereby ending the apparently interminable wrangling over the School Certificate which the Norwood Report produced.

The prevailing view in the Ministry continued to be that public examinations would diminish in importance. In 1952 it stated in a circular that 'it appears to be quite unnecessary for nationally attested certificates to be made available on the same scale as in the past'.[21] But even as this circular was issued, work was going forward to establish a new examining body to run a form of GCE which would be particularly adapted to meet the needs of technical schools and colleges. Much of the detailed work in creating this body was undertaken by the City and Guilds Institute but it was the support given in the SSEC by the AEC which led to the establishment of the Associated Examining Board. In 1954 it submitted its draft regulations to the SSEC for approval. This was the first non-university based examining board and for this reason it was particularly welcome to those in the LEAs and the AEC who had felt a certain jealousy or suspicion towards the influence of the university-based boards on the curricula of 'their' secondary schools.

Dissatisfaction with '0' level of the GCE was centred in the early 1950s on the standard required to pass. This had been raised to the level required for the old grading of 'credit' in the former School Certificate. The schools and some LEAs came to press for a lower grade of pass since many candidates who would have achieved at least a modest level of success in the School Certificate now got nothing. Moreover some authorities expressed the growing desire for an examination at a level which the more able pupils in secondary modern schools could take and some such as Northumberland developed their own leaving certificates. From 1953 the evidence indicates that the Secretary to the AEC believed there was a need for a leaving examination for the good average pupil – 'the average of the whole age group and not of grammar schools'. The NUT agreed to join the AEC in a joint working party to consider the issue and in 1954 urged the Minister to set up a committee of inquiry. The Minister did not reply to the request and early in 1955 the AEC pressed for an 'urgent inquiry'.[22]

The aim of the AEC was a completely new examination suited to the pupil of average ability and not under the control of the university examining bodies – thus a lower level pass in the GCE would not meet the aim. The Ministry resisted the pressure and in July 1955 responded by saying that a new nationally recognised examination for modern schools would induce uniformity of syllabuses, curricula and methods at stages and ages where uniformity was most undesirable. Moreover success in such an examination might become an index to the efficiency of schools and this would be both unrealistic and oppresive in view of the wide differences in the circumstances of the schools themselves.[23] For the next two years the pressure was sustained by the AEC and by teachers' associations and it continued to be resisted by the Minister and his advisers.

An increasing number of LEAs began to plan regionally recognised examinations and leaving certificates while independent bodies such as the Royal Society of Arts and the College of Preceptors met an increasing demand from modern schools for publicly recognised examinations. In 1957 the Ministry tried to refer the issue to the Crowther Committee which was then working on its inquiry into the education of the fifteen to eighteen year olds. This would remove the matter from the SSEC where the LEAs were influential and it would remove the matter from the persuasive personal pressure of Alexander who was seen as an effective and vigorous advocate of the new examination inside the SSEC.

The replacement of Lord Hailsham as Minister by Geoffrey Lloyd and the departure of Sir John Wolfenden from the chairmanship of the SSEC and his replacement by Dr J F Lockwood, Master of Birkbeck College, London, opened the way for some movement. After a meeting of the SSEC on 28 March 1958 at which great pressure had been exerted to achieve movement, the new chairman wrote to the Minister asking him again to appoint an *ad hoc* committee of inquiry at an early date and added a threat from the Council to go it alone,

> some members of the Council feel so strongly on this issue that it seems likely that at their next meeting they will, in default of an alternative, propose the appointment of a sub-committee from amongst their own members, with such additions as they may think it necessary to make by cooption, to undertake an immediate investigation of the problem.

In his reply the Minister defended the position taken by his predecessors, but added that if the Council wished to conduct a study of the problem of examinations below GCE '0' level, he would not wish to stand in their way.

Initially the sub-committee which the SSEC established consisted of six members including Robert Beloe, the Chief Education Officer for Surrey as Chairman, and Alexander. The setting up of the Beloe Committee may be seen in retrospect as a crucial stage in the development of national policy. The Committee recommended an examination to meet the needs of the next 40 per cent of each age group – assuming that the most able 20 per cent would take GCE '0' level. Regional boards – not universities – were to be responsible for conducting the new examination. In the spring of 1961 the SSEC considered the report of the Beloe Committee and recommended the Minister to accept its proposals. In July the Minister told the Commons that he had decided reluctantly to accept the recommendations.[25]

At the time that these events were taking place, thoughts were developing among civil servants within the Ministry that would have had the effect of strengthening the Minister's impact on all curriculum issues. It was the function of LEAs simply to secure that enough suitable schools were provided for their areas and to maintain them effectively. The Minister's function was to develop and apply sound policies including specifically educational policies such as teaching methods, subjects, curricula, examinations, internal school organisation and the use of staff within schools. A policy-making organ needed to be created within schools branch to undertake this task. It would take the form of a full-time development group to be headed jointly by a staff inspector and an assistant secretary.[26] The Beloe proposals clearly needed more work to make them practical and within the Ministry they seemed to offer the chance for the new machinery to be created and to start operating in the field of curriculum and examinations.

In February 1962 Derek Morrell who had developed successful and cooperative relations with LEAs in the architects and building branch was moved to schools branch to assume responsibilities in connection with examinations. When the announcement of the formation of the curriculum study group – the name given to the development group – was made, Morrell was named as joint head along with an inspector. In March the Permanent Secretary, Mary Smieton wrote to local authorities' and teachers' associations telling them that the Ministry was establishing a study group concerned with the curriculum and examinations. A 'team' was being formed to deal with Certificate of Secondary Education (CSE) examination matters and would be concerned with advising the SSEC. By way of reassurance, she stated that the new unit would not impinge as the responsibilities of the SSEC but merely perform a service function.[27] In a speech subsequently the Minister also reassured teachers and local authorities that the existing pattern of powers would not be disturbed.

The possible consequences of the creation of this new unit within the Ministry soon began to cause fears among the other partners who came to see this as an attempt to secure ministerial control over the curriculum. The AEC pressed the view that the group should be put under the guidance of a body representative of LEAs and teachers' associations as well as the Ministry. In October the AEC sent a deputation to the Minister, Edward Boyle, to argue this case. He agreed to give further consideration to the matter.[28]

Some thought was given to ways of dealing with the issues involved and there was some contact between Morrell and Alexander. Morrell sent Alexander a copy of a paper he had written about a proposed Schools Council for the Curriculum and Examinations and invited him to comment on it. This paper discussed the problem of control of the curriculum and put forward for discussion a council with sixty members from teachers' and local authority associations, the universities and industry which would replace the SSEC and have a much wider field of responsibility.[29] By the summer the time seemed ripe for a meeting of teachers' associations and local authority organisations. The Minister presided over this but it was held at the NUT headquarters, Hamilton House, to lessen any impression of Ministry domination. The meeting expressed fully the fears of Ministry control of the curriculum but did agree to a working party to explore the position further. The chairman was J F Lockwood, chairman of the SSEC and Master of Birkbeck College where meetings were held. Both Morrell and Alexander were members of the working party. The CCA, AMC and London County Council representatives perhaps expressed reservations most strongly to what they saw as Ministry proposals. The working party went over the ground which had been covered in informal exchanges the previous winter. Morrell after close consultation with Alexander again wrote the crucial paper proposing a dual organisation which shared control between LEAs and teachers' associations and made detailed proposals in finance and staffing. In order to avoid the suspicion and antipathy which some members of the working party felt towards anything from the Ministry, it was arranged that Alexander should put in the revised proposals in his name. He was able to argue the case as presented vigorously and persuaded the working party to accept the proposals in November at its third meeting.[30] At this meeting the constitution, financing and staffing arrangements for the new Schools Council were all agreed and it was also decided that the Curriculum Studies Group should come to an end and that its members should work directly under the Council with an independent secretariat.

There remains on the file an interesting exchange of letters after this meeting between Morrell and Alexander. The former wrote to the latter congratulating him on his masterly handling in the meeting of the paper on the constitution. In his reply Alexander wrote to express his admiration for Morrell's ability to sit completely silent while another argued the case for the paper he had written.[31] When *The Report of the Working Party on the Schools' Curricula and Examinations* was published early in 1964 it was prefaced by a statement from the Minister welcoming the proposals. Before the end of the year the Schools Council held its first meeting. The influence of the AEC had been crucial in bringing the Council into existence. The disappearance of the Schools Council and the assertion of control over the curriculum and examinations by the Secretary of State twenty years later would have hardly been conceivable if education committees had still possessed any effective national organisation.

Committees and their officers

The growth of the maintained education system from the later 1940s meant that the responsibilities of each education committee and its officers increased steadily. The composition of the statutory committee has been discussed elsewhere and while individual constitutional changes were made by different authorities for particular reasons, the general pattern of categories of membership has remained stable. The sub-committee arrangements of LEAs are, of course, modified as may seem most expedient from time to time and were widely refashioned after 1944 to accommodate the abolition of 'elementary' schooling as such and to facilitate the handling of the wider variety of services which education was expected to provide. The extent to which members of the education committee involved themselves in comparatively detailed business seems for many years to have followed local tradition. In the West Riding, for instance, the tradition of involvement by members was much stronger than in the counties generally. In the 1960s Alec Clegg pointed out to his members that in many other counties the education committee and its sub-committees worked on a three monthly cycle whereas such meetings were held monthly in the West Riding. He commented that the 'extraordinary intensity of meetings . . . is due to the determination of the Committee to reserve to elected members decisions which might fittingly be dealt with by a member of staff'. A calculation quantified the committee effort needed in the county to administer education. This showed that there were some 600 committees consisting of 9,000 members which met on approximately 3,700 occasions each year.[32]

The expansion of the school system, higher expectations about standards, the provision of far more further education opportunities and a rapid growth of various supporting services meant that more administrative staff had to be appointed to manage bigger and growing businesses. An example of this was that school meals for LEAs became large catering organisations with about 75 per cent of pupils taking school dinner. It has been shown that between 1951 and 1959 the average number of graduates recruited to local educational administration each year was twenty-six while the average for the years 1960 to 1965 grew to fifty-three. The total number of professional administrative posts in local education administration increased from 802 in 1951 to 961 in 1961 and to 1,264 in 1971.[33]

The role of the chief education officer was of crucial importance in the post war expansion. His traditional function was set out by A L Binns thus '. . . the duty of the chief education officer is twofold; he should advise his employers fearlessly and competently on all educational matters coming before them for decision, and having given his advice he should carry out the instructions of his employers cheerfully and efficiently whether or not his advice has been taken.'[34] While all chief officers were concerned to ensure that the machinery operated smoothly and efficiently, the evidence suggests that many saw themselves as having a strong professional commitment to educational objectives and that this involved finding ways of improving the content and quality of the education service. Again many have seen themselves as innovators. George Taylor, for instance, in his period of service as chief education officer for Leeds, regarded innovation and the introduction of new ideas and new objectives as a necessary part of his duty. He has related how surprised some councillors were when they learned of the extent to which innovations came from within the office. It is difficult to generalise about the influence of chief education officers over policy, but it does seem that they have at least been much more obviously influential where a broad consensus existed between the political parties or where independent councillors carried weight locally. The generally accepted need for educational advance in the post-war years was much suited to giving the able and thoughtful chief education officer his opportunity to develop and improve the maintained system in ways which a professional would perceive and desire.[35]

Some education officers established their reputations at the national as much as – or perhaps more than – in the locality. Robert Beloe of Surrey, John Newsom of Hertfordshire, Lionel Russell of Birmingham all gave their names to government reports during these years. Alec Clegg became one of the foremost national figures as an authority on educational issues. Lincoln Ralphs was county education officer for Norfolk from 1950 to 1973. At the time of his retirement it was reported that he ran Norfolk by doing all the work between five and seven o'clock in the morning and then left his instructions for his staff to carry out while he caught an early train to London for a day of committees. One of his London-based responsibilities was to chair the Schools Council and that must certainly have required a good deal of time and energy.[36] Almost invariably the chairmen and members of education committees encouraged their officers to become involved in affairs at the national level. Lionel Russell recorded that when he became chief education officer for Birmingham in 1946 the chairman advised him 'for the sake of our authority to take some part in national work'.[37]

The executive of the AEC included both members and officers and in that respect was unlike some other local government organisations. It was the ready availability of expertise within the AEC which often made its advice of particular value to the Ministry. The Secretary of the Association built up a close working relationship with senior civil servants. The arrangement worked well and both the CCA and AMC generally accepted the AEC as the lead organisation in dealings with the Ministry of Education and in the Burnham Committee where Alexander succeeded Sharp as secretary to the authorities' panel and as joint secretary to the Committee. There was a brief flurry of concern in 1946 when the CCA and AMC complained to the Permanent Secretary that their associations had not been consulted before a circular was issued. This produced some discussion within the Ministry. At that time the committee on school sites and building procedures was at work and so was a working party on the licensing of theatrical children. The minutes which passed between civil servants included the comment that

> If for those working parties we frequently call upon Dr Alexander, that is because his wider experience and interest are specially valuable, and not because he represents the AEC rather than the AMC or any other body. Also his extensive and constant contacts with education officers all over the country put him in a specially good position to offer informal advice and to explain to them the procedures which are the outcome of the working parties.

Even if the views of the AMC and CCA could have been obtained and reconciled without too great delay they would have been of little assistance on what was workable and practical.[38]

The system of statutory education committees with expert administrative officers working under them and with a small but energetic central organisation played a crucial role in giving reality to many of the aspirations which the Education Act of 1944 embodied. In this way the sad disappointments of the years following the Fisher Act of 1918 were avoided.

References

1   PRO., ED 46/155, Postwar educational reconstruction, M S Holmes, 5 Nov. 1940.
2   PRO., ED 136/212, R S Wood to Holmes, 8 Nov. 1940.
3   E Percy, *Some Memories*, 1958, p. 122.

4 PRO., ED 136/639, Holmes to Young, 2 Nov. 1938.

5 PRO., ED 136/238, Sylvia Goodfellow to Holmes, 27 Mar. 1942; Note by R.A.B. on a meeting of the AEC attended with Chuter Ede, 6 Nov. 1942; Note from Holmes to Butler and reply, 29 Dec. 1942.

6 PRO., ED 136/460, Cropper to Butler, 28 Jan. 1944; Butler to Cropper, 4 Feb. 1944.

7 PRO., CAB 128, Cabinet conclusions, 16 Jan. 1947.

8 AEC, C59(c), correspondence with Nottinghamshire Education Committee, Jan. 1946; I am indebted to John R Dunford for this reference and for drawing my attention to some of the material which follows in his doctoral thesis 'A study of the influence of the Association of Education Committees on school building policy in England and Wales 1944–1964' (Leeds, 1984).

9 PRO., ED 150/151, 9 and 27 April, 1 and 8 May, 6 June 1946.

10 J R Dunford, op. cit., p. 72; AEC, C59(c), Minutes of School Sites and Building Committee and correspondence, July – Oct. 1946.

11 AEC, C59(c), Minutes of 20 and 27 Sep. 1946; Ministry of Education, Report of the Committee on *School Sites and Building Procedures*, 1946 sections 6 and 7.

12 Stuart Maclure, *Educational development and school building: aspects of public policy 1945–73*, 1984, p. 30.

13 AEC, B111(b), D M Nenk to Alexander, 14 Mar. 1952.

14 PP, 1952–53, Eighth Report from the Select Committee on the Estimates, 20 May 1953.

15 Ministry of Education, Circular 283, Dec. 1954.

16 AEC, B157(a), Alexander to Eccles, 2 Mar. 1956.

17 AEC, A19c, Morrell to Alexander, 23 June 1961.

18 Quoted by J R Dunford, op. cit., p. 385; *Social Trends*, No. 2, 1971 Table 134.

19 A full study of this is 'The influence of the Association of Education Committees upon the development of secondary school examinations in England, 1943 to 1964' (University of Leeds, Ph. D. thesis, 1979) by Peter Fisher and I am indebted to this research. A briefer version of the thesis has been published under the title *External Examinations in Secondary Schools in England and Wales, 1944–1964* by the same author and published by the University of Leeds Museum of the History of Education in 1982.

20 AEC, 85E4, Draft circular, 15 Feb. 1946; Williams to Secretary AEC, 15 Feb. 1946 and subsequent correspondence; PRO, ED 147/133, Interview memorandum, 29 Apr. 1946.

21 Ministry of Education, Circular 256, 4 Sep. 1952.

22 AEC, C56(a), Alexander to Fletcher (Ministry), 11 June 1954 and subsequent correspondence on this file.

23 Ministry of Education, Circular 289, 9 July 1955.

24 AEC, B153(a), Lockwood to Minister, 3 Apr. 1958; Minister to Lockwood, 17 June 1958.

25 Hansard, H C, DCXLIV, 909–12 (17 July 1961).

26 Edward Boyle Papers. Memorandum, *The work of the schools branch: a new look*, T.W., Oct. 1961.

27 AEC, A511, Mary Smieton to Alexander, 9 Mar. 1962.

28   AEC Executive Committee Minutes, 255, 29 Nov. 1962.
29   AEC, A31a, Morrell to Alexander, 21 Feb. 1963 and draft memorandum.
30   *Ibid*, Curriculum and Examinations Working Party papers, 1, 2, 3, 4, 5 and 12a; Morrell's secretary to Alexander's secretary, 19 Nov. 1963; CEWP minute 3. 27 Nov. 1913, paras. 8 to 14.
31   AEC, A347a, Morrell to Alexander, 28 Nov. 1963; Alexander to Morrell, 29 Nov. 1963.
32   West Riding Education Committee, Policy and Finance Sub-cttee, memorandum from the Education Officer, 5 July 1968; WREC, *West Riding Education: Ten Years of Change*, 1954, p. 135.
33   V C Greenhalgh, 'Local educational administrators, 1870–1974; the emergence and growth of a profession' (University of Leeds, Ph.D. thesis, 1974) p. 253. Chapter VIII of this thesis contains a useful discussion of the profession since 1944.
34   A L Binns, 'The CEO and his Task', *Journal of Education*, April, 1957, p. 140.
35   See V C Greenhalgh, op. cit., pp. 264–70, for a discussion of this matter and evidence.
36   *TES*, 6 June 1973, p. 112.
37   L Russell, 'The CEO and his masters', *Education*, 8 Nov. 1968, p. 685.
38   PRO, ED 136/807, W R L to Permanent Secretary, 16 Jan. 1947.

Chapter 4

Growing difficulties, local government reorganisation and the end of the Association of Education Committees

Introduction of block grant and subsequent developments

The steady increase in expenditure which was required to bring about the main reforms in the Butler Act – especially the provision of secondary education for all and the additional demand which this created for higher education – perhaps inevitably led to the education service becoming a more central political issue as the reformed system grew. The politics were sharpened by the economic position in this country. While the British economy recorded a much improved rate of growth in the quarter-century following 1945 than it had done in the previous twenty-five years, the faster growth of comparable industrial countries cast its shadow over Britain's development. Looking back on this, Alec Cairncross has pointed out that 'the shortfall in Britain hurt national pride and seemed to defy explanation'.[1] Part of the justification for increased spending on education had been that it made a vital contribution to economic growth. The general acceptance of this idea in the main political parties had played its part in building up and sustaining the general consensus of support for the implementation of the principal Butler reforms. Thus as the relatively disappointing economic performance became increasingly apparent, recent developments in education themselves began to be regarded with suspicion. Contention grew among the politicians and the public as to the value or otherwise of what some came to describe as an 'expensive' or even 'extravagant' education system.

At the local level the education interest has found it more difficult to sustain its claim on the resources required to operate the system because of a fundamental change in the method of financing the service which was enacted in 1958. From the early years of the twentieth century the central government's main financial support for education had taken the form of specific grant and had been based on a system of meeting a certain percentage of the approved actual expenditure of LEAs. In the 1950s the education grant had met about 60 per cent of authorities' outgoings. As shown above, Treasury hostility to the percentage grant was not new. It had tried to abolish the system in 1922 at the time of the Geddes economies committee and again in 1933 with the Ray Committee. In evidence which it presented in 1922 the Board of Education considered the percentage system to be probably the strongest and most effective instrument the government could possess for maintaining educational standards. The Treasury's aims in 1957 were, firstly, to reduce the total level of government grants to local government since they had overtaken the total of rates and this was 'a patently unhealthy development'. Secondly, since 1939 the yield from direct taxes had grown sixfold while rates had only doubled even though personal incomes (after income tax) had on average nearly trebled. More of the cost of local government should, therefore, be borne by the rates.[2] In the Commons, the Minister of Housing and Local Government, Henry Brooke, argued that a general grant in place of the specific, percentage grants would avoid detailed central supervision and that the Exchequer would have a surer knowledge of its commitments in advance. 'Our aim is to foster and stimulate a vigorous and independent local government, and to give members of councils a greater incentive to take a lively interest in their local expenditure by placing much more of it under their own control'.[3] The government's proposals were not welcomed by many local government bodies and were strongly opposed by the AEC and teachers' associations. The AEC and NUT ran a joint campaign against them with meetings in various towns and strong lobbying. Given the terms of the Education Act of 1944, either the conception of a national policy for education was to be abandoned or the greater control over expenditure which the government proposed to give authorities was illusory. In a percipient paper which he prepared for the Association of Chief Education Officers, George Taylor of Leeds pointed out that the immediate consequence of the new arrangement with a block grant was that the Minister would lose the flexible control essential if he were to ensure the efficiency of the national system. The powers he would have to rely on – possibly under sections 68 and 99 – were clumsy, slow and inappropriate; indeed subsequent court decisions appear to have illustrated this. He also believed that the government proposed to rely on a series of financial yardsticks related to average costs. The effect of this would be to restrain the more energetic authorities with a consequent progressive reduction in the average costs and an inevitable reduction in the general level of standards – a process of 'progressive reaction'. From the Treasury's standpoint a general grant was clearly preferable because the achievement of a saving under a percentage grant system involved an open and direct policy decision, whereas a block grant could easily be controlled by the Exchequer without embarrassment to a government's declared policy. In the longer term Taylor feared that the new system would lead to an increasing variation in the standards of the educational provision between LEAs, with the denial of the basic principle of the 1944 Act that educational opportunity should be independent of place of birth. 'If these fears are well-founded, it is the local authorities on whom the criticism will fall, and it would indeed be ironical if the introduction of a block grant, ostensibly designed to strengthen local authorities, ultimately led to a nationalised or regionalised system of public education.'[4]

It was in fact the sheer cost of the 1944 reforms which gave the Treasury the opportunity to end the percentage, specific grant in 1958. The need to increase and maintain a large school building programme in the later 1950s during Eccles' first period as Minister meant that the Treasury had to be persuaded to agree to a high level of capital investment if there was to be a place in a secondary school for every child over the age of eleven. The Under-Secretary for Finance and Accountant General in the Ministry was David Nenk and he was principally responsible for reaching an understanding with the Treasury by which it would undertake to see that the capital programme would be sustained if the Ministry in its turn would not oppose the Treasury's plan for a block grant system.[5] Thus the Local Government Act of 1958 changed the grant system and, initially, the new arrangement did not have any significantly adverse effect on the education service. The service had to grow to deal with the increased number of pupils and students. Lord Alexander wrote in 1976 that the consequences that he had feared in the late 1950s . . . 'did not occur until recent years. Prior to that monies were fairly readily available and I do not think education suffered.'[6] On the other hand the disappearance of the separate grant certainly served to feed the notion that education was simply a local service like any other rather than a national service to be provided evenly throughout the country as a whole. By the time of local government reform in the early 1970s this idea had become widespread and the DES was to have some difficulty in keeping a system of education committees which represented more than local political groupings.

In the general grant calculations expenditure on education represented a very high percentage of the total. The Local Government Act of 1966 was designed to amalgamate the general grant with a number of other specific grants (such as highways and rate deficiency) in a new and broader rate support grant, thereby taking the process which began in 1958 rather further. The outcome of these measures is shown in table 4.1.

Pressure on local authority budgets really became significant following the oil price crisis in 1973–4. In a budget statement in December 1974 the Chancellor asked authorities to limit any increases in expenditure for the coming financial year to developments that were absolutely unavoidable. Detailed advice in the field of education was issued by the DES in Circular 12/74. This explained that the grant settlement took into account the expected increases in the number of students and pupils but it did not include any provision for expanding peripheral services nor for any developments in response to reports recently issued by advisory committees such as English language provision (Bullock Report), in-service teacher training (James Report) and adult education (Russell Report). From 1975 the central government's support grant for local authorities began to decline as a percentage of their expenditure even as growing economic difficulties produced increasing disillusion and sharpened political divisions.

Table 4.1 Local Government Grant and Expenditure 1959–1976.

Year	Expenditure on Education (£m)	Total relevant expenditure (£m)	Grant	Educational Expenditure as % of total rel. exp.	General grant as % of total rel. exp.
1959–60	597	707	402	84.47	56.82
1960–61	648	766	429	84.65	55.96
1961–62	718	850	472	84.51	55.49
1962–63	809	952	519	84.91	54.46
1963–64	891	1078	587	82.68	54.41
1964–65	955	1160	625	82.37	53.88
1965–66	1106	1337	736	82.71	55.03
1966–67	1206	1480	810	81.47	54.71
					Rate support grant as % of total rel. exp.
1967–68	1321	2618	1283	50.48	48.99
1968–69	1418	2793	1395	50.78	49.94
1969–70	1597	3143	1619	50.82	51.50
1970–71	1779	3593	1880	49.53	52.32
1971–72	2084	4115	2173	50.64	52.80
1972–73	2408	4735	2528	50.86	53.39
1973–74	2828	5714	3155	49.50	55.21
1974–75	3318	6888	4384	48.17	63.65
1975–76	5118	9986	5788	51.25	57.96

Comprehensive schools

Perhaps the most important of the educational issues to bring an end to consensus was that of the form of secondary schooling. This became an increasingly important political party issue from about 1965 and in some ways it may be surprising that politicians did not fall upon this as a contentious party issue earlier. Even in 1941 when senior officers of the Board of Education were planning the post-war school system, William Cleary, head of elementary branch, urged on his colleagues that 'the obvious and perhaps the only satisfactory answer is the multilateral post-primary school attended by all children over eleven alike, most of whom will stay to fifteen, many to sixteen, and a few later.' For political and social reasons he believed that common schools for all from the age of eleven would eventually be inevitable. The total war of democracy against dictatorship was emphasising the essential unity of the nation. It would lead inevitably to a greater merging of the different sections of the community and the breaking down of social and economic barriers and privileges. Thus the common school was 'the only full solution of the problem of a truly democratic education'. The difficulty of trying to move to this arrangement with the existing comparatively small school buildings and the need not to wait for ever for 'the New Jerusalem' led Maurice Holmes, the Permanent Secretary, to turn towards what became the tripartite system.[7] Subsequently the political pressure foreseen by Cleary only finally became significant twenty years later when a secondary place had been provided for most children on tripartite lines. It was then that parents whose children had been sent to secondary modern schools experienced the feeling of 'relative deprivation' in sufficient numbers for their grievance to attract increasingly strong support from among the politicians and for the Labour government eventually to attempt new legislation on the issue of secondary school organisation.

In practice during the twenty years following the Second World War the Ministry of Education had only permitted common or comprehensive schools where there was a growing secondary school age population in need of new accommodation and leaving existing grammar schools largely untouched. As the White paper of 1958, *Secondary Education for All: A New Drive*, pointed out it was most likely that conditions would favour the setting up of comprehensive schools in new towns or rural areas hitherto lacking facilities rather than in established urban areas. Thus while the LCC was failing to get approval for comprehensive schools, the West Riding under Conservative control from 1955 to 1958 was able to open comprehensives at Colne Valley, Penistone and Tadcaster. Moreover, even if the claims that pupils could be sorted with any real accuracy into grammar schools and modern schools at eleven were being rebutted with increasing frequency, by the mid-1960s many LEAs had just about provided a place in a secondary school for every child after a tremendous effort to reorganise and build new schools on the tripartite system. Thus when the pressure built up to carry through another secondary school reorganisation, the reluctance shown by some LEAs was no doubt reinforced by the feeling that they had only just completed this struggle and were reluctant to start again.

The White Paper of 1958 had given a very qualified endorsement to comprehensive schools but Edward Boyle subsequently pointed out that when he returned to Curzon Street as Minister in 1962 it was clear to him and to the senior officials that support for the development of education along comprehensive lines had been gaining momentum. Within the Ministry it was estimated that in 1963 ninety out of 163 LEAs had in a few cases completed or else were working on comprehensive school schemes for the whole or a part of their areas. The policy of 'overlap' between grammar and modern schools contained in the 1958 White Paper was no longer adequate since, as one chief education officer put it, 'there is still no overlap in parents' minds'. Too many secondary modern schools were socially one class schools and too obviously the bottom schools in their areas. Ambitious parents could not be expected to react philosophically to the news that their children had failed to pass into something better.[8]

When the Labour government came into office in 1964 there was no immediate break in the 'consensus' attitude towards secondary schooling. The next year Circular 10/65 was still hortatory although by 1966 pressure was being applied to reluctant authorities. The understanding attitude of the opposition spokesmen on education, Edward Boyle and William van Straubenzee, in the mid-sixties meant that there was no immediate major clash. The Enfield cases in 1967 when the Secretary of State's actions over reorganisation were twice successfully challenged in the courts by ratepayers and parents led to the passing of the Education Act of 1968 to broaden the discretion of the Secretary of State in considering changes in the nature of a school. The Enfield affair and subsequent legislation served to raise the temperature of conflict.

The government had found itself having considerable difficulties from 1965 with a number of LEAs including Surrey and Cheshire, but both Crosland and Prentice were able to make enough general progress towards comprehensive schooling to enable them to resist pressure from their own backbenchers for new legislation. There was a natural and proper reluctance among many officers concerned with running the schools to take sides with contestants in the local squabbles which took place and the files of the AEC show that from time to time education officers sought advice on their difficulties from the Association. An organisation which included all education committees in its membership (apart from the ILEA) and which paid no regard to the party affiliation or non-affiliation of any of its members could clearly make no value judgements on an issue of party political controversy. In writing to an education officer who had approached him in 1969 the Secretary pointed out that local authority associations had traditionally supported the view that each authority had the right to determine the organisation of schools in its own area. He added

> but I do not think our people would continue to defend an organisation which involved selection of 25 or 30 percent going to grammar schools and the remainder to modern schools. I think our people have probably reached the point where they accept that this is socially divisive and is probably not the best organisation of secondary education.[9]

But the very progress made in bringing forward comprehensive schemes served to stimulate opposition to them. The loss – or prospective loss – of good sixth forms with high academic attainments annoyed many parents who were not wealthy but did mind about academic standards. Then the actual schemes for setting up comprehensive schools without much in the way of new building too often involved botched-up arrangements with one large school using buildings perhaps two or three miles apart. Yet other schemes involved the fragmentation of sixth-form resources. The fear also gained ground that egalitarianism was being put before standards in education. This fear was certainly fed by enthusiastic progressives who argued that streaming, setting or ability grouping of any sort had to be abolished in the interests of avoiding distinctions between pupils. Finally the first of the Black Papers was published in 1969, written largely by those who believed that sheer hard effort was being insufficiently valued and that progressives were setting aside the necessary function of academic education in validating and upholding professional standards.[10] The appointment of Edward Short as Secretary of State for Education and Science in 1969 was seen by some as a sign of the government's determination to overcome this growing opposition and to force through total comprehensive reorganisation.

The attempt by local authorities to maintain that they had the right to decide their form of secondary school organisation soon produced a breakdown in the relationship between the AEC and the Secretary of State which contrasted remarkably with the close relationship which had existed for much of the previous quarter of a century. In January 1969 Short told a press conference on the building programme that it was characteristic of local authorities that they did not look at their costs too carefully and attacked them for their extravagance. The immediate issue was the cost of additional building to meet the added numbers who would be in the schools with the raising of the minimum leaving age to sixteen. *Education* commented that

> How much harm Mr Short has done and is doing to his own position, as the champion of the education service, by turning an occasion for celebration into an episode in his financial tangle with local authorities can only be guessed. There can be no doubt that Tuesday's demonstration of ill-informed prejudice did nothing to enhance his reputation . . .[11]

The government included a bill to promote universal comprehensive schooling in its programme outlined in the Queen's Speech in the autumn of 1969. The AEC affirmed that it was not concerned with whether comprehensive schools were good or bad but with the relationship between central and local government in the organisation of the education service. It had debated this issue twenty years earlier and concluded that each LEA should determine the organisation of secondary education for itself. It therefore made representations to the government urging it not to legislate in the way intended. One fear which educational administrators expressed was of the chaos which would ensue if school organisation became the subject of adversarial party politics with attempts to change the form of organisation each time there was a change of government. This looked a likely outcome of Short's bill since the opposition had given an undertaking to repeal the measure when it took office. An exchange of letters between Short and Alexander after the AEC's memorandum had been criticised by the former perhaps serves to illustrate the extent to which the Secretary of State and the AEC held strongly contrasting presuppositions from which no harmony was likely. Alexander explained in his letter that the political affiliation of members had no significance in the Association, that it was most anxious that the education service should not be harmed in a situation in which extreme was countered with extreme. He added that the Executive Committee was as dismayed at the prospect of the Act being repealed by a Conservative government as it was by the possibility of it becoming law under a Labour administration since both would harm the development of the service and damage the sympathetic cooperation which existed in the majority of areas. In his reply Short pointed out that all spheres of national policy were subject to the effect of changes in government, both local and national. 'Like you, I should deprecate any part of the education service becoming a political football, but it would be quite wrong for the government of the day not to act in accordance with its own convictions'.[12] Two letters on this same file a little later serve to indicate the consistency of the Secretary's attitude. In reply to a request for his views on a controversial pamphlet by Rhodes Boyson published by the National Education Association, Alexander replied that he would not be inclined to pay too much attention to the pamphlet. 'I think the urgent need here is to avoid party political polarisation'.[13]

The outcome of the general election in 1970 ensured that Short's bill was not enacted. The arrival of Margaret Thatcher at the DES also led quickly to the withdrawal of the circular advocating comprehensive schools and during the next four years proposals for such schools were examined much more critically even although the broad movement towards comprehensivisation continued steadily as may be seen in Table 4.2.

Table 4.2 England and Wales: comprehensive schools and pupils

Year	Total secondary		Comprehensive		Percentage of pupils attending comprehensive schools
	Schools	Pupils	Schools	Pupils	
1965	5,863	2,819,054	262	239,619	8.5
1969	5,468	2,964,131	976	777,082	26.2
1970	5,385	3,045,974	1,250	973,701	31.9
1971	5,295	3,143,879	1,520	1,183,703	37.6
1972	5,212	3,251,426	1,777	1,412,174	43.3
1973	5,159	3,362,554	2,137	1,703,671	50.6
1974	5,079	3,723,743	2,677	2,310,103	62.0
1975	5,035	3,826,646	3,069	2,666,992	69.6
1976	4,982	3,935,500	3,387	2,976,408	75.6
1977	4,988	3,938,863	3,594	3,226,890	81.9
1978	4,962	4,093,032	3,901	3,436,637	83.9
1979	4,938	4,113,698	4,047	3,559,611	86.5

Initially the new Secretary of State believed that reliance on local autonomy would serve to check the growing power of the state and produce a mixed system of secondary schools. When local autonomy seemed not to be producing a mixed system, and since coercion was out of the question, local autonomy came to be redefined in terms of parents rather than elected representatives and Section 13 procedures seem to have been so adapted. This in itself produced a certain strain on the central-local partnership. In 1973 the AEC made representations to the Secretary of State about the use of Section 13 provisions and Alexander wrote of the Association's concern in his 'Week by Week' column.[14]

The collapse of the education consensus and the major clash over comprehensive reorganisation between the Labour and Conservative parties came at times to dominate educational affairs in the later 'sixties and 'seventies. It played its part in drawing education committees into the centre of local political conflicts and helped to undermine their national association and influence. The depth of feeling over this issue was perhaps illustrated by an incident which occurred after Edward Short left office. *The Times* reported that he had suggested teachers should consider refusing to cooperate in the 11-plus examination if in any area it continued under the new Heath government. The 'Week by Week' column in *Education* pointed out that for an ex-Secretary of State to suggest to 'teachers that they should virtually be guilty of mutiny must, therefore, be regarded as a most irresponsible statement'. The person who had taken a completely authoritarian attitude himself while in office now appeared to suggest that if teachers found themselves in disagreement either with national or local authority policy, they should be guilty of mutiny.[15]

The change back from Conservative to Labour administration in 1974 meant that universal comprehensive schooling again became a central government objective. Circular 4/74 was duly issued which revived, reaffirmed and updated the contents of Circular 10/65. LEAs were asked to inform the government of their proposals to eliminate selection and complete reorganisation. Following local government reorganisation there were 105 LEAs and of these 67 said they expected to complete secondary reorganisation by 1980, 31 committed themselves to comprehensive reorganisation in principle subject to the availability of resources while the remaining 7 indicated that they would only reorganise if compelled to do so. A new Bill was introduced into the Commons reviving Edward Short's failed Bill of 1970 and it received the Royal Assent in November 1976. The AEC continued to oppose such legislation and in a letter to Fred Mulley, by now Secretary of State, Alexander also suggested that a fully comprehensive system was well on the way to evolving without compulsion. In his reply Mulley argued that legislation was essential since public opinion only followed in the wake of reorganisation.[16] There was determined opposition to the measure from certain authorities, Tameside's opposition perhaps being the best known. Inevitably after the Conservatives won the 1979 election a new Education Act was passed reversing the requirements of Mulley's 1976 measure.

The conflict over the organisation of secondary education certainly played a major part in sharpening political conflict in education and in making it more difficult for statutory education committees with outside non-party members to continue their traditional relationship to their parent councils. In any case growing political polarisation of the Conservative and Labour parties, both apparently being moved away from the centre by right- and left-wing activists, would have made it more difficult for education committees to have sustained their customary position either locally or nationally through the AEC. Ironically it was after one divisive issue, religion, had largely been overcome in the education system that more purely political and social issues came to have an increasingly sharp impact. The creation of statutory education committees with nominees from the contending religious groups on them might have seemed to be one way of handling the central conflict in education in 1902 and of keeping it out of the machinery of local councils generally. Following the settlement embodied in the Butler Act, these issues have caused much less contention in the period following the Second World War.

Local government reorganisation

It was against this background of increasingly bitter political division that the long-discussed and foreshadowed reorganisation of local government took place after nearly thirty years of Royal Commissions and committees of inquiry. For reasons suggested above, it took place at a time when the interests of education within local government itself were already under something of a shadow while the professional organisations among teachers were much less united and less effective than they had been. Those who were evidently opposed to the whole post-war system were finding an effective means of attack through appealing to the figure of 'the parent' – classless, non-ideological and seeking no more than a fair deal for the child.

The only significant change in the pattern of local government between 1945 and 1974 was in the London area. For many years education had been the responsibility of the London and Middlesex County Councils, the counties bordering on London (Kent, Surrey, Hertfordshire, Essex) and the county boroughs of Croydon, East Ham and West Ham. The Royal Commission on London Government in 1960 proposed the creation of the Greater London Council to cover the whole of the London area with fifty-two boroughs. Education was to be the responsibility of the GLC which was to devolve much of the work to the fifty-two London boroughs. The Ministry of Education feared that education was the one service which the new structure would not fit and that the pattern of large conglomerate authorities and executive authorities working under them would also subsequently be taken as the pattern to be applied nationally. The Ministry contacted the AEC urging it to submit its views to the government; it also contacted other educational organisations including the NUT and the Joint Four Secondary Associations with the same request. The AEC duly submitted a critical memorandum on the proposals making a number of points which suggested that the practical difficulties involved in the double authority scheme were likely to prove very great. It had been proposed, for instance, that one authority would appoint teaching staff while the others would have the right of dismissal. The White Paper differed from the Royal Commission in proposing fewer and larger London boroughs with populations of 200,000 or so and with education entirely as a borough service over most of the London area. The area of the former London School Board and later of the LCC would have caused problems if broken up in this manner with an enormous amount of inter-authority travel by pupils and transfer payments between authorities. As a body under more or less permanent Labour control the LCC education committee had been something of a thorn in the flesh of successive Conservative governments. Nevertheless it seemed more suitable to keep this central area as one unit rather than to risk the administrative confusion of division. Hence the Inner London Education Authority was set up as a special committee of the GLC and consisting of members of the GLC from the central boroughs, along with one representative from the City and from each of the inner London borough councils. The reforms in the London area took effect in 1965 following the London Government Act of 1963. Each of the new borough authorities had its education committee on traditional lines and all of these joined the AEC. The ILEA, like its predecessor, remained the only education committee in England and Wales outside of the Association.[16]

The reform of local government in the London area went through in the early 1960s without difficulties arising over the position, standing or operation of education committees. It was some indication of the change in the national standing of the education system between the early 1960s and the early 1970s that the continued existence of statutory committees came under threat by the time that local government reorganisation was undertaken in the rest of the country.

In 1966 a Royal Commission was set up under Lord Redcliffe-Maud to examine local government outside London and to recommend reforms. The Royal Commission produced a set of recommendations which would have established single or one tier authorities throughout the country to discharge all executive functions. There were to be exceptions to this pattern in the Manchester, Birmingham and Liverpool districts which were to have two-tier systems with an overall authority rather like the GLC and district councils, similar to London boroughs. While the Labour government accepted the report's recommended pattern early in 1970, the Conservative Party sought to preserve the historic shire county system and was returned to office a few months later pledged to establish a two-tier system. Early in 1971 the Environment Department, now under Peter Walker, issued a White Paper outlining the system to be adopted and arguing a case for it. Change was needed because there were too many authorities which were too small in area and resources to do their work efficiently. Moreover the separation of county boroughs from counties had created artificial barriers between the bigger towns and their hinterlands while the efficient administration of local government functions needed to embrace both town and country. In future authorities were to be large enough in population and resources to meet administrative needs. For such functions as education and the personal social services, populations ought broadly to be in the range 250,000 to 1,000,000 – although such limits were not to be regarded as 'inflexible'. Local authority personal health services were to go to the National Health Service while water supply, sewerage and drainage was to go to newly created *ad hoc* bodies.

There were to be six urban or metropolitan counties, Merseyside, South-East Lancashire and North-East Cheshire, West Midlands, South Yorkshire, West Yorkshire, Tyne and Wear. In these education and personal services would be administered by district councils, elsewhere they would be the responsibility of county councils. Responsibility for libraries was to rest with education authorities. In the shire counties the White Paper emphasised that education 'must be the undivided responsibility of the county authorities'. It followed that 'it is the intention to end the provisions for schemes of divisional education by which local education authorities are compelled to delegate certain of their functions to divisional executives'. Similarly, excepted districts were to have no place in the new local government structure. One important reason for emphasising the need for counties to have undivided responsibility for education was to avoid situations in which former county boroughs which became district councils could press for the effective delegation to them of education powers, thereby undermining the aim of bringing together the bigger towns with their hinterlands.[17] Outside of the metropolitan areas, forty-seven county boroughs lost their corporate identity as local education authorities. Most of these fell outside of the population limits set out in the White Paper, but a number of the largest would on population grounds taken alone have met the criterion. These included Teesside (411,000 population), Hull (290,000), Stoke-on-Trent (270,000), Nottingham (300,000), Leicester (276,000), Plymouth (256,000), Bristol (426,000) and Cardiff (284,000). At the other extreme, thirty-one of the county boroughs which were to cease from being LEAs had populations of between 50,000 and 150,000.

Of the new districts in metropolitan counties, eleven had fewer than the stated minimum population of 200,000. Three of these were in the North East and were centred on Tynemouth, Gateshead and South Shields; another three were in the expiring West Riding and were centred on Halifax, Barnsley and Rotherham. Not only were some of these rather small in population terms, they also lacked the financial resources which might have served to compensate. From the viewpoint of the education service, 250,000 was in any case apparently on the low side. In its evidence to the Royal Commission the DES had recommended that for education purposes an authority should have at least 500,000 although it would have gone as low as 300,000 in sparsely populated areas. The CCA had recommended 500,000 while the AEC had put the minimum at 400,000. The creation of new local education authorities as small as the eleven which failed to meet even the criteria set out in the White Paper caused some concern among educational administrators. The West

Riding prepared a paper which applied the usual indices of educational need and of family poverty to the new authorities. This showed that by rateable value per head of population the three poorest education authorities in England would be the Yorkshire metropolitan districts of Kirklees, Calderdale and Barnsley.

At the national level the paper illustrated that the north would have 60 per cent of the new authorities below 500,000, nearly 80 per cent of those below 300,000 and over 80 per cent of those below 250,000. In the south there were none at all in the latter two categories and only four in the midlands.[18]

Correspondence on the AEC files indicates that the DES shared fully their concern over the smallest of the new LEAs. The Permanent Secretary apparently 'would welcome all the pressure that can be brought to bear against establishing eleven of the metropolitan districts, on which he shares our views completely', Alexander wrote to Clegg and added 'I gather the Department did their best with Walker, but Walker was adamant.'[19] The pressure mounted by those interested in education failed to change these proposals.

Quite apart from issues concerning the size and number of LEAs, the position of education within the local authority structure had become a matter for debate. Michael Heseltine, then a junior minister at the Environment Department, addressed the July meeting of the Society of Education Officers in 1971 and a number of questions were raised by members. In his replies he could see no reason why anyone from education should be on the committees looking into the future organisation and management structure of local government. He also questioned whether it was really the case that the statutory position of education committees was so necessary.[20] The working group which was set up to advise on future organisation consisted of six local government officers and one 'outside' member. The chairman was M A Bains, clerk of Kent County Council and there were three other clerks, two treasurers and the company secretary of ICI. It included no one concerned with or experienced in administering the services to the public for which local government bodies were created. Hence there was heavy emphasis on local government as a corporate being which apparently existed for its own sake. Local councils were unfortunately not viewed as the public sees them, as local providers of nationwide services.

In August 1971 preliminary proposals of the Environment Department itself on the internal organisation of local authorities were circulated to the relevant organisations. These showed that in accordance with the Department's current policy of strengthening the corporate management and corporate decision-making it proposed that statutory requirements for local committees should only be retained for police and national parks. After an interval the statutory requirement for education committees was to be abandoned so that authorities might have full discretion to arrange their committee structures unhindered. Moreover the statutory requirement for an education officer was to be dropped also so as to permit authorities full flexibility in deciding the extent to which they should or should not continue this post or combine its functions with some other.[21] Comments were invited which were to be considered by the Bains Committee. The AEC sent in its comments setting out the reasons why there should be statutory education committees and education officers. The final date for comments was 8 October but three days later the interim report of the Bains Committee was circulated to the press ready for publication on 12 October. This document went rather further than the Environment Department's proposals had done in seeking to abolish the legal requirements to appoint any named committee. It maintained that this practice encouraged departmentalism, with committees behaving as though they were independent of the council and of each other. Statutory requirements for the appointment or governing the dismissal of particular officers should also be dropped. If councils could not be trusted to behave reasonably, they could not be regarded as the right bodies to provide services.[22]

The various bodies from the world of education felt a sense of outrage on two counts, their arguments had apparently not even been considered by the Bains Committee since it had prepared its interim report without waiting for them and there was no sign of any attempt being made to understand the position of education in local government and the necessity to involve outside interests including both the churches and the teaching profession. The AEC made vigorous protests to the Bains working group itself, to the DES and alerted other educational bodies to the dangers opening up in front of the education system.[23] At this stage the churches, the teachers' organisations, the AEC and education committees all made clear to the government their very strong feelings on the need to preserve the essence of the arrangements which had stood since the beginning of the century with the statutory requirement for education committees which included coopted members representing, for instance, the considerable interests of the Church authorities and others in the schools. The Church of England General Synod sent very strong representations to the Environment Department. Since education was above all a personal service, the arguments for keeping an identifiable committee with an identifiable officer carrying overall responsibility for the service 'would seem difficult to refute. In the circular they are not refuted. No attempt seems to have been made to marshal them at all.' In particular, the suggestion that the conditions which originally gave rise to the special need for statutory treatment had changed or vanished 'would seem to be almost the opposite of the truth'. It was only the close cooperation which the statutory committee system produced which had enabled the progress since 1945 to be achieved.[24]

In replying to a letter from one chief education officer who forwarded a letter he had received from the director of education for a Roman Catholic Diocese inquiring who was really behind the move to get rid of statutory education committees and 'who are the people – rather than the position – that I should be watching', Alexander felt that the main pressure for abolition came from the AMC while within the government the danger came from people in the Environment Department and from Peter Walker in particular.[25] During the campaign against abolition of the statutory committee, copies of much of the correspondence sent to the Environment Department had been sent to the Permanent Secretary at the DES. In a note to Alexander in late October he wrote that the only comment he could make was that on the face of it the whole thing seemed to be a most extraordinary chain of events, adding that Ministers had certainly heard other views apart from those of the Environment Department's working group.[26]

When the Bill came to be published the representations were seen to have been effective. The essential provisions relating to the education service had been secured with a statutory education committee and the appointment of a chief education officer. Alexander sent a congratulatory letter to Margaret Thatcher, then Secretary of State, 'on having secured in the Local Government Bill the essential provisions relating to the education service.'[27] In a letter on the same theme to Pile, the Permanent Secretary, Alexander added that the representations would be sustained lest any attempt be made to move amendments to the Bill. He also expressed some disappointment that some of the small metropolitan districts which were really too small to administer education were being retained –

although this was much less important than the main issue. A flavour of the intensity of the struggle within the government over this was, perhaps, given by Pile's reply. 'No one will deny that it was quite a battle – and a nice one to win. There may, as you rightly surmise, be counter attacks during the passage of the Local Government Bill, but I believe the government will stand firm.'[28]

The Bill made its way through the legislative process in time to receive the Royal Assent in 1972 with no essential change in the provisions concerning education. Following consultations the DES issued a circular of guidance on the impact of the new Act on 'the education function' in local government. So far as the new councils' education committees were concerned, their constitutions would need to be approved by the Secretary of State before they could be set up and early ministerial guidance on constitution and membership was promised. The statutory requirement for the appointment of a chief education officer was retained but the approval of the short-list by the Secretary of State before any appointment was made was no longer to be a requirement. In fact this provision which had been inserted in the 1944 Act on the initiative of Chuter Ede, had been a dead letter. There is no record of the Minister, or later the Secretary of State, forbidding the appointment of any individual. The circular also pointed out that while education committees could not set up sub-committees on an area basis and delegate functions to them, they could if they wished establish officers to discharge their functions on an area basis and appoint any area committees on a purely advisory basis.[29] The further guidance on the membership of education committees indicated that the Secretary of State would look for between a quarter and a third of the members to be coopted and the new authorities were particularly asked to include members nominated by the teaching profession and the churches as well as 'members with knowledge and experience of industry and commerce, agriculture and the universities'.[30]

The implementation of the local government reorganisation did give rise to considerable anxiety both in education committees and in the DES over the way in which some of the new authorities appeared to be narrowing what they would consider as education business and by proposing the removal of certain essentially education matters from the education committee in spite of the 1972 Act's requirement that no function in respect of education could be discharged by any committee other than the education committee or one of its sub-committees. The issue arose at Stockport where the council wanted to set up a 'recreation and culture division' in which it proposed to locate its youth service. Although the DES confirmed that all youth service provision made under the Education Acts must be the business of the education committee, Stockport apparently sought to persist.[31] The General Secretary of the General Synod Board of Education wrote to ask the AEC's advice on the efforts being made by the new county councils in Avon and Gloucestershire to remove youth work from their education committees and put it under parks and leisure. The National Council of Social Services also made representations to the AEC, the CCA and AMC over the disquiet it felt over the allocation of youth service matters to committees not specifically concerned with education.[32] In some places responsibility for non-teaching staff was given to personnel committees and in others the lack of adequate delegated powers created problems. The prevalence of the corporate management notions in the early 1970s did produce a number of such difficulties in different parts of the country. The DES certainly did what it could to support the position of education committees. Indeed in a letter to Alexander in July 1973 Pile assured him that there would be 'no diminution in the Department's support (witness the Whitehall scars we bear) for the continued existence of strong and influential education committees throughout the country.'[33]

End of the national organisation of education committees

In retrospect Pile appears to have been much too optimistic when in the context of the reorganisation problems which confronted education he wrote that in the Department they did not believe 'that, in general, there is any real danger of the scope and influence of education committees being diminished.'[34] Even though the ideas associated with the 'corporate management' style which strongly influenced the Maud and Bains Committees were seldom applied in this extreme form, nevertheless they had considerable general influence on attitudes in quite a number of the post 1974 local authorities. In the investigation which he undertook into policy making in local education authorities after 1974, Jennings showed the extent to which policy and resources committees had been set up and that their preeminent function was control of finances and the budget making process. In those authorities where this was combined with strong political control by a single party, there were 'multiple opportunities for controlling and shaping the policy process through decisions by the policy and resources committee'. At the same time in these authorities policy was effectively decided by the controlling party group and was then simply taken through the various committees. Where there was no strong single party control, the policy and resources committee tended to debate the requests from the various service committees and to recommend priorities between them to councils.[35] Partly stimulated by the controversies of the 1960s over the form of secondary organisation, political parties at the local levels were moving towards the domination of policy making in education in an increasing number of authorities well before reorganisation. The reorganisation marked a considerable step forward in that process. Indeed, in some of the new and artificially contrived areas that were put together as authorities and which lacked any sort of historical feeling of unity, such as Humberside, Avon, Kirklees and Calderdale, the political parties provided some of the very few linking agencies which could quickly come together. In the increasingly party political local authority, the statutory education committee consisting partly of coopted non-councillors was bound often to count for less. In some places the only circumstances in which it has been able to function in its originally intended form has been where the council itself has been 'hung' – in other words where no political party has had a majority and effective decision making has returned to the formal constitutional structure.

Against this background the probability of a place being found in the reorganised local government world for a national association which represented education committees on a non-political basis looks in retrospect to have been remote. Nevertheless when the extensive reorganisation had been set in train there were hopes that one organisation could be established to represent all of the new local authorities and that the AEC could have formed some part of that organisation. The decision to abandon the mainly single tier arrangements proposed by the Maud Commission and to preserve counties and districts in a national two-tier structure led to the preservation of the urban Association of Municipal Corporations and the more rural County Councils Association and their transformation into the Association of Metropolitan Authorities and the Association of County Councils. The much more far-reaching party politicisation of local government by the 1970s probably made a single organisation impractical in any case and the AMA was fostered and built up particularly by Labour local government politicians largely from the bigger county boroughs and the London area where the party found much of its support. The much greater Conservative strength in the counties led to the ACC in its turn being under the control of Conservative influences until 1985.

When the government reenacted the provision for statutory education committees with their degree of cooptative membership it accepted the view that the efficiency and smooth working of the education system required the involvement in the government and administration of elements from the community other than party politicians – including representatives of the churches, of teaching, of industry and agriculture. Experience had shown that committees so constituted had had a particularly crucial and beneficial effect on the development of education policy at the national level through their association on a strictly non-party political basis. The continuation of this influence was clearly dependent on the tacit willingness of the local politicians to accept that in the field of education they should stand back sufficiently to permit a national organisation to continue. Clearly many of those who were influential in the AMA did not believe this and some influential voices on the other side in the ACC shared their view. Thus although there were discussions and negotiations at various levels over a period of about four years, eventually the national organisation for education committees was squeezed out.

The series of meetings, discussions and exchanges of correspondence on the future of the AEC from 1972 was lengthy and it is not possible to follow the detail here. In March 1974 the *Times Educational Supplement* published quite a full account of the events of the 1973–4 winter.[36] The formal position of the existing main local authority associations had crystallised by 5 April 1973 when their leaders agreed 'to recommend the future authorities not to agree to central organisations for any single function until decisions are made about the federation'. From this time the eventual ending of the AEC in its existing form became the policy of the conservative counties' organisation as well as of the Labour dominated AMA. The formal invitation to the education committees of the new authorities to join the AEC in late summer of 1973 were countered by a circular letter from A C Hetherington, Secretary to 'the Meeting of Representatives of the new county councils' to the new chief executives stating that 'it would not be appropriate for new county councils or one of their committees to consider joining at the present

time any proposed central organisation for a single function'.[37] The
NUT fully realised the difficulties likely to beset the education
service if the education committees lost their national voice. It sent a
letter to all chief education officers for their authorities to consider
stating that it was essential that at national level there should be a
body able to speak for all LEA education committees so as to present
the needs of the education service as seen by these committees and
which could maintain the relationship with the teaching profession
which had been developed by the AEC over many years.[38] The AEC
and the many members of education committees from both large
parties who still wished to see the Association continue, found
themselves under pressure to conform to the negative official line of
the AMA and ACC. In these circumstances the attitude of the
government as expressed by the DES became significant politically.
Sufficient support from that quarter might possibly have saved the
Association.

Towards the end of 1973 the oil crisis and then the coal strike led
early the next year to a general election and the return to office of the
Labour Party. The likely consequence of this for the AEC's national
position might, perhaps, have been surmised from a report of a
speech in 1973 by Edward Short, the last Secretary of State in the
previous Labour government. He addressed himself to the issue of
local authority associations and found particular problems arose over
the AEC which had given education a strong voice nationally. But
'the strong voice had often been a reactionary one' and during the
period of the Labour government it had been far from friendly. The
AEC, he said, was not democratic since it was dominated by officers
and this was to the detriment of education. Moreover education
might gain by being looked at by an association which looked at a
wider field of services such as housing, planning and social services
since 'thinking about education in recent years has moved towards a
view of it in its social context'.[39] The most significant official
patronage in the hands of the government was membership of the
Burnham Committee. In line with the attitudes which they had
adopted, the AMA and ACC sought the removal of the AEC from
that committee and approached the new Labour Secretary of State,
Reg Prentice.

The critical decision seems to have been made at the end of March
or in April 1974. An urgent letter sent by hand to the Permanent
Secretary at the Department by Alexander set out the case for the
AEC's continuing membership. It pointed out that the Burnham

Committee had been set up on the initiative of the AEC half a century or so earlier, that the Association had provided the secretariat and accommodation for the authorities panels for over fifty years. Its claim to remain representative was based on three points. Firstly that despite pressure from the AMA and ACC, the number of committees in membership was greater than the total number of local authorities in the ACC. Secondly the population represented by the membership of the AEC was greater than the total population represented by the AMA including London. Thirdly the AEC remained the most widely representative of all the bodies since it included English and Welsh counties, metropolitan districts and London boroughs.[40] In May Prentice wrote to inform the AEC that he had decided to remove it from the Burnham Committee as from September 1974. The reason for the decision was stated to be that responsibility for education within local government lay with the local education authorities themselves and not with their education committees. In law this had been the position since 1902 but hitherto the Board, Ministry and then Department of Education had chosen to emphasise the importance of the statutory committee and, indeed, fought and won the battle to uphold this position in 1972. By early 1974 the attitude of DES ministers had changed and although some of the DES senior officers have in recent years lamented the passing of a national voice for the education committees, after the loss of its place on Burnham, it really became impossible for the AEC to gain enough members in the new environment for it to survive.

The AMA and ACC set up what Short had described as a 'simple joint unit doing servicing' and known as the Council of Local Education Authorities (CLEA). This was not in any sense a national organisation for education committees. The AMA and ACC each has its own central committee for education which reports only to its parent body. The Council meets regularly and holds an annual conference. Policy decisions can normally only be taken where there is no significant political difference of view since the leader of the AMA or the ACC present at any meeting can always reserve the taking of a decision to his particular association. While the members of CLEA may sit on education committees, they do not represent them but their parent authorities. Moreover education officers cannot be members. In 1975 and 1976 there were protracted discussions around the issue of a merger of the AEC with CLEA, but by early 1977 these were clearly going to be unproductive and the AEC formally disbanded, transferring its assets to a charitable trust with a small Board of Trustees. The publishing company was sold to Longman Group Limited and the continued publication of the Association's journal *Education* was assured.

Thus the local education authority service moved into the difficult and dangerous years of the later 1970s and 1980s without a single, effective, national voice – with consequences for education and local government which are considered further by George Cooke in the chapter that follows.

References

1 A Cairncross, *Years of Planning*, 1985, p. 499.
2 Conservative Research Department, 'A summary of the government's proposals', 19 June 1957, circulated to Conservative MPs.
3 Hansard, H C, Vol. 564, pp. 1078–80. (12 Feb. 1957).
4 Brotherton Library Archives, LEA 485, Association of Chief Education Officers, 'The government's proposal to introduce a general grant', June, 1957.
5 Interview, Lord Boyle, 7 Mar. 1979.
6 AEC, A1152, Lord Alexander to M L Franks, 16 Dec. 1976.
7 PRO, ED 46/155, Postwar social development and its effects on schools, W Cleary, 13 Jan. 1941; ED 136/217, M Holmes to R S Wood, 3 Mar. 1941.
8 Lord Boyle, 'The politics of secondary school reorganisation: some reflections', *Journal of Educational Administration and History*, IV, 2, 1972, p. 32.
9 AEC, A1113, Correspondence between Robinson (Southport) and Alexander, 20 and 27 Oct. 1969.
10 Cox, C B and Dyson, A E *Fight for Education: a Black Paper*, 1969, and subsequent issues.
11 *Guardian*, 22 Jan. 1969; *Education*, 24 Jan. 1969.
12 AEC, A1113, Alexander to Short, 24 Apr. 1970; Short to Alexander, 4 May 1970.
13 Ibid., D H Wilcoxson to Alexander, 15 July, 1970; Alexander to Wilcoxon, 26 July 1970.
14 Roger Woods, 'Margaret Thatcher and secondary reorganisation', *Journal of Education Administration and History*, XIII, 2, 1981, p. 59; *Education* 7 Sep. 1973.
15 *Education*, 3 July 1970.
16 AEC, E74, Alexander to Mulley, 27 Feb. 1976; Mulley to Alexander, 17 Mar. 1976; AEC, A518, Telephone message from M A Walker,

Ministry of Education, 29 Nov. 1960; letter Walker to Alexander confirming message, 29 Nov. 1960.

17 Dept. of the Environment, *Local Government in England: Government Proposals for Reorganisation*, [Cmmd. 4584], 1971. Dept. of the Environment, Circular 8/71. Welsh office, *The Reform of Local Government in Wales: Consultative Document*, 1971.

18 AEC, A1065, County Council of the West Riding of Yorkshire, Local Government Reorganisation, March 1971.

19 AEC, A1065, Alexander to Clegg, 22 Apr. 1971.

20 *Education*, 16 July 1971.

21 Department of the Environment and Welsh Office, Statutory provisions affecting the internal organisation of local authorities in England and Wales, 26 Aug. 1971.

22 Department of the Environment, Interim report of the working group on local authority management, 16 Sep. 1971.

23 AEC, A1065, Alexander to Secretary of the Working Group on Local Authority Management Structures, 13 Oct. 1971; other correspondence on this file with NUT, Joint Four, Society of Education Officers, Church of England Board of Education, Catholic Education Council, NAHT, etc.

24 AEC, A1065, Revd. George Whitfield (Church Board of Education), to J E Hanningan (Dept. of Environment), 29 Oct. 1971.

25 AEC, A1065, Alexander to Clegg, 15 Nov. 1971.

26 AEC, A1065, Pile to Alexander, 26 Oct. 1971.

27 AEC, A1065, Alexander to Mrs Thatcher, 8 Nov. 1971.

28 AEC, A1065, Alexander to Pile, 8 Nov. 1971; Pile to Alexander, 10 Nov. 1971.

29 DES, Circular 1/73, 16 Jan. 1973.

30 DES, Circular 8/73, 29 Mar. 1973.

31 AEC, A1101, C G Davey to Alexander, 19 Jan. 1973 and subsequent correspondence.

32 AEC, A1101, George Whitfield to Alexander, 3 Apr. 1973.

33 AEC, A1101, Pile to Alexander, 5 July 1973.

34 AEC, A1101, Pile to Alexander, 28 June 1973.

35 Robert E Jennings, *Education and Politics: policy-making in local education authorities*, 1977, pp. 54–6 and 174–7.

36 *TES*, 1 Mar. 1974.

37 AEC, K3, Copy of letter from A C Hetherington among papers for meeting of Executive Committee on 28 Sept. 1973.

38 AEC, K3, Copy of letter from Edward Britton, General Secretary of the NUT to all chief education officers, 10 Oct. 1973.

39 *Labour Councillor*, Vol. 1, No. 1, 1973, p. 7.

40 AEC, C21d, Alexander to Pile, 25 Mar. 1974.

PART II

Chapter 5

Increasing problems

George Cooke

After six years war service in the army as an infantry and staff officer and five years teaching history at Manchester Grammar School, George Cooke entered educational administration in the West Riding of Yorkshire in 1951 under Sir Alec Clegg. He was subsequently Assistant Director in Liverpool and Deputy Director in Sheffield before becoming Director of Education for Lincolnshire (Lindsey) in 1965. On local government reorganisation, he was County Education Officer for Lincolnshire from 1973–78. He was President of the Society of Education Officers in 1975 and General Secretary of the society from 1978–84. He has a long-standing and continuing interest in special education. He was made a CBE in 1978.

Introduction

The 1974 reorganisation of local government in England and Wales, which soon afterwards brought in its train the end of the AEC, was avowedly designed to strengthen local government and to improve the services for which it was responsible. There were some who felt and expressed doubts at the time – the messy nature of the reorganisation itself and the simultaneous removal of school and community health and water services from local authority control did not exactly inspire confidence. But the doubts were roughly overridden by the government of the day, and after the event there was a very general determination to make the new system work well for the simple but sufficient reason that there was no immediately available alternative. Yet, little more than a decade later (autumn

1985), the doubts seem to have been amply justified. A major component of the new structure (the Greater London Council and the six metropolitan counties) is about to be abolished; the once great city of Liverpool staggers on the edge of bankruptcy and chaos; local government generally appears to have become progressively weaker, more divided and more apprehensive under the onslaught of aggressive centralism; and the public education service within local government is more criticised, more disrupted and less happy within itself than at any time since the 1939–45 war. There is much talk of 'crisis' in local government and education, and it is frequently said in relation to both that morale has never been lower. Further radical reorganisation of local government is being urged as the only hope of preventing its continuing decline and eventual supersession.[1] And in education central government quite clearly sees its role as increasingly interventionist and believes itself far more capable of improving the quality and cost-effectiveness of the education service than the LEAs, the institutions and the professionals if left within broad limits to themselves. These events are all inter-connected. Of course, they are due in large part to factors external to both local government and education – party politics at national level; economic recession and retrenchment; industrial conflict; social and technological change; and so on – but they are also certainly due in part to the stresses and strains, errors and omissions within local government and education. They raise in acute form the questions whether strong, democratic, local government of any kind really is a necessary part of late twentieth century democratic Britain, and whether, if it is, the education service should have a place in it or should be run by central government from Whitehall through whatever consultative and administrative machinery, regional or local, it cares to establish. These are not academic issues. They relate very directly to the future nature and health of our society. For all its failures and broken dreams, education is about the future and touches every aspect of our lives. It is 'the friend of those who seek a more efficient, more open and more just society'.[2] Decisions taken, or not taken, in the next few years about who runs it, how it is run, for what purposes and towards what ends, will produce many of their more important consequences in the next century. And certainly, if education were to become a 'nationalised' service fully under central government control, that would generate a whole range of new problems and anxieties very different from but not necessarily any easier (indeed potentially more dangerous) than those which torment us now; and it would change for better or worse the whole atmosphere and 'ethos' of the service.

Central government has been involved one way or another in the provision of public education in England and Wales for just over 150 years. For more than half that time, the management and development of the education service (excluding the universities and the independent schools) has been increasingly and since 1944 overwhelmingly the responsibility of the local education authorities (essentially, the counties, cities and boroughs, working through statutory education committees) within a decentralised system which in more recent times has been generally if somewhat loosely described as a 'national system locally administered'. Neither central nor local government was directly involved in the beginnings and early growth of public education provision, which was rather the result of many voluntary and often very local initiatives over many years by the churches, charities and philanthropic individuals. The state intervention, which began in 1833 with a modest financial grant to the voluntary providing bodies, soon increased to a point where it was causing sufficient concern in central government quarters to produce the cutbacks and controls of the Revised Code of 1862. So a period of relative enlightenment and generosity on the part of central government was followed by a period of tighter control and retrenchment, and a pattern was set which is perhaps inescapable in any major welfare service always hungry for more resources.

The subsequent history of the development of the education service has been told many times and appears again in an interesting new light in the preceding chapters which clearly illustrate how early the key problems of controls and relationships were identified. Few generalisations are possible in this context, but perhaps one that is safe is that, once the new local education authorities had been established in 1902, central government (though it certainly had its more 'active' periods and at times energetically used its powers to direct, inspect, guide and encourage) did not until comparatively recently seek to exercise close control over the detailed operation of the service. Rather it was content to leave considerable areas of discretion to the local education authorities and to the governing bodies and professional staff of individual schools and colleges. Central government, as we all used to explain patiently to foreign visitors, did not build or own the schools, employ teachers, or prescribe curricula and textbooks. There was the statutory framework of laws, regulations and instruments/articles of government; there were government policy documents, circulars, administrative memoranda and other official communications; there were HMI reports; and – very significant for the LEAs – there were certain key controls exercised by central government over finance, building allocations and standards, and numbers of teachers in training and available for employment. But the principle of 'partnership' between central government, local education authorities, voluntary providing bodies, institutions, professional staff and their representative organisations was not seriously challenged. Shipman[3] has rightly said that the partnership image has about it 'a cosy reassurance' which inadequately explains the harsher realities, the incoherences, tensions and horse-trading that were also part of the system, but he also describes it as 'a gentle relationship' and adds, in words with which many of those most closely involved would readily agree, 'At the start of the 1970s, national and local interests were still compatible'.

What then has changed? Quite simply, within the last ten years or so, there has developed within the education service and in local government generally a growing fear that central control is increasing beyond all reasonable limits to a point at which 'partnership' becomes meaningless. If that is true, it ought to be a matter of the greatest public concern. It is, of course, perfectly possible to argue that the fear is exaggerated and the display of panic in local government circles largely artificial and politically inspired. And it is certainly reasonable to accept that central government has its own very substantial and entirely proper part to play in the partnership, that it has had its more active, interventionist periods before, and that in a period of acute economic difficulty and financial stringency there may well be a need for more central controls. It is also possible to argue that central government has no deliberate policy to upset the partnership and is merely stepping in when forced to do so by the manifest weaknesses and failures of the education service and local government to grapple successfully with the urgent problems that face them. But that too should be a matter of public concern, not least because it raises questions about the extent to which those weaknesses and failures are the proper responsibility of the education service and local government or have themselves been created or accentuated by central government and could be remedied by them.

Central government might well take the argument from the proposition that retrenchment inevitably means more central controls and that contraction in the education service provides the opportunity for a national drive towards better quality, relevance and utility, to the further proposition that earlier ideas based on partnership and cooperation are outmoded and that our long-cherished decentralised system has become an obstacle rather than an asset. But the latter case has not so far been made, at any rate publicly. The real concern, therefore, in local government education circles is that the effectiveness of the education partnership is being undermined whilst the principle of partnership continues to be upheld by virtually everybody concerned. It is one thing to have a centralised education service as a matter of deliberate choice; it is quite another thing to have a so-called decentralised system which no longer commands confidence and is gradually becoming more and more centralised as it were by default. The present situation pleases nobody. It is 'neither satisfactory nor stable'.[4] There are probably very few knowledgeable people in the education service these days (and not many in local government either) who, if their memories stretch that far, do not regard the 'fifties and 'sixties as a kind of 'Golden Age' of optimism, commitment and comparative harmony in stark contrast to present-day feelings of anxiety, disillusionment and soured relationships. Few would deny that, whatever the causes, in the early 1970s (and significantly about the time of local government reorganisation in 1974) a lot of things changed for the worse for the public services generally and for education in particular, and that they have not really recovered since. What is surely now beyond dispute is that, if a healthy education service and a healthy system of local government are regarded as essential components of our kind of free, democratic society, the present situation cannot simply be allowed to slide steadily downhill into the twenty-first century.

The remainder of this book considers further the nature of the education partnership, the case for continuing it, the changes that might be needed to maximise its chances of success if it is continued, and the possible alternatives to it if it is not continued. It must be said, of course, that administrative systems do not of themselves guarantee success in educational terms, but good administrative systems can contribute towards, and bad administrative systems can certainly militate against, such success. And it must be admitted that there is little taste just now in education or local government circles for further radical reform unless it is clearly seen to be absolutely necessary for survival. The memories of the traumas of earlier reorganisations are still fresh in many minds. But perhaps it is a question of survival? If further radical reform of systems and attitudes seems to be the only alternative to continuing and more rapid deterioration, then surely it must be attempted – or at any rate openly and urgently discussed. Too many of the new local government leaders after 1974 paid scant attention to the early warnings they received that things were far from well, and recklessly sacrificed much of their strength and support in the pursuit of short-term political and personal advantages. There are some signs now that more perceptive and constructive approaches are gathering strength, but time is short and the dangers are very great. It would be sad indeed if local government in Britain were to be effectively destroyed because its supporters could not agree on their objectives and could not stop quarrelling amongst themselves.

The 1944 Act and the 'Partnership' concept

The case for division of powers

Throughout the whole of the forty years following the 1939–45 war, there was hardly any time when reform of or adjustment to the system of local government was not in one way or another under active consideration. The actual reorganisations (of the Greater London area in 1965, of the rest of England and Wales in 1974 and of Scotland in 1975)* did not stop but rather intensified the argument. In the course of that long-drawn-out debate, the general case for elected local authorities – in terms of counterbalancing excessive central power, providing for the 'practice of democracy', responding to the diversity of local needs, ensuring the accountability of local officials, and so on – has been stated and re-stated many times, in recent years very cogently by Jones and Stewart.[5]

The case for the education service in particular to be within the elected local authority system is, if not unique, certainly unusually compelling, and relates as much to the nature of the education service itself as to wider constitutional issues. In 1973, in a re-markably prescient public statement on 'The Education Officer and the Structure of the Education Service in Local Government', the Society of Education Officers (SEO) argued strongly for the

* Northern Ireland received separate and different treatment in the reorganisation of 1973 which created five non-elected Education and Library Boards.

partnership principle and proclaimed themselves 'all local government men', but at the same time they set out in nineteen
'principles' the conditions necessary in their view for education to
remain secure and happy within local government and made clear that
they were not 'local government men at any price'. In retrospect, it is
peculiarly ironic that so little attention was paid at the time by local
government to its education officers, and that only four years later the
AEC, which brought together elected members of various political
persuasions and their education officers in equal membership of a
national organisation designed to provide a single, effective national
voice for the education service in local government and to argue
consistently from that position, was also brought to an untimely end.

Nevertheless, the case for elected local authorities of some kind to
play a major role in managing the public education service, within a
system which recognises fully the other interests involved, remains
strong. It rests essentially on half a dozen key propositions. There is
first the argument that the 'division of power' between elected central
and local government (with certain important areas of decision and
discretion reserved also for the governors, heads and staffs of schools)
is a fundamental safeguard of freedom in our kind of parliamentary
democracy and an effective bulwark against overweening central
power. The essential point for education (which it is easy to overstate
and dramatise) is that any political group which wished to destroy
democracy from within using methods more subtle than brute force
would need sooner or later to take over not only the armed forces, the
forces of law and order and the communications network, but also the
education service. In other words, a decentralised education system
provides some, albeit limited, protection against tyranny, whether
overt or masquerading in democratic guise. Writing within a decade
of the end of the 1939–45 war, Lord (then Dr) Alexander[6] had no
doubts on this score; he identified the distribution of power as 'the
first principle and perhaps the most important principle on which the
English system of education rests' and added that 'when Hitler came
to power in Germany the fact that he could determine what was taught
in the schools of Germany was perhaps the most important factor in
creating and consolidating the Nazi regime'. Other more recent
writers with shorter memories have tended to play down this
argument. Thus Shipman:[7]

> The panic over central government strength can be exaggerated. . . . Of
> course there is a fear that an authoritarian government could attempt to

control the curriculum, select teachers and censor textbooks. The outcry against what looked like the first tentative steps to examine the curriculum in the late 1970s was a healthy warning. But many other democratic rights would have to be lost before a government could control the content of education in Britain. It is right to be vigilant, but it is also necessary to be balanced. Central government acts for democracy as well as being a possible threat to it. Some extended influence could be beneficial. Historically central government has often acted to raise standards of provision and to secure some consistency and equality among local communities.

There is truth in that too, but it is surely right to add a further note of warning. Men and women of balanced views must surely remain very vigilant indeed, these days. Balanced views tend to be swept away when the dominant voices in public life represent the kind of 'conviction politics' which go beyond the energetic pursuit of strongly held beliefs and emerge as insufferable arrogance, total absense of self-criticism and an unwillingness to accept moderation, mediation, compromise or reconciliation.

The second argument is perhaps more difficult to state with confidence now than it was ten, twenty or thirty years ago. It is simply that the system works and that no other system is likely to work better. The achievements of the 'partnership years' will be discussed briefly later on, but there can be no doubt that they were real and very considerable. In 1973, the SEO was able to assert confidently, almost arrogantly,

> Despite some disappointments and a chronic shortage of resources in relation to public demand and need, the system has worked well over many years and has achieved an astonishing expansion and diversification of the education service, which has been (and in many important respects still is) a model for the rest of the world. The system is quite capable of developing in a dynamic way to meet the challenge of the years ahead.

Such statements would not be so confidently made today after more than a decade of retrenchment, contraction, mounting criticism and falling morale, but there are still, or at least were until very recently, observers less obviously partisan than the SEO who point to the smooth efficiency with which the education service is generally run with only occasional crises and those mostly the result of external pressures and confrontations. Thus, Alan Alexander (1982)[8], while conceding that the local government system in general has few defenders and fewer enthusiasts and that 'the overwhelming impression is of practitioners, both members and officers, whose determination to make the system work owes more to a wish to avoid a further reorganisation than to a commitment to the systems that arose from the legislation of 1972 and 1973', nevertheless asserts that 'Children continue to be educated, dustbins to be emptied, houses to be built and home helps to be organised; or, if they do not, the reasons are more likely to be concerned with financial stringency than with the failure of the local government system to work'. Shipman (1984)[9] speaks of the administration of education as a 'triumph of organisation' which runs with 'few painful hiccups'; he pays tribute to the efficiency, commitment and skill of the administrators and professionals and adds 'Ten million people use the service each year and it runs with only occasional disruption'. Even the government White Paper *Better Schools* (1985)[10] whilst stressing how much still remains to be done, concedes that 'There is much to admire in our schools. . . . Over the last thirty years, the system has expanded and adapted. . . . There have been marked improvements in both primary and secondary education'. And it is as well to remember that much of the education service bears little resemblance in the eyes of those who know it best to the frightening picture so often and so eagerly presented by the media, and that there is very little evidence so far that alternative approaches directly controlled by the centre have any magic formula (other than resources denied to the local authority services) by which to resolve current problems.

The third argument is that in education, as in other human activities concerned mainly with people rather than things, there are very few 'right' answers which stand unchallenged over long periods of time. By its very nature education is concerned with reconciling the irreconcilable and with preserving a delicate and shifting balance between conflicting objectives. Nowhere is this more apparent than in the tension between the perceived needs of the community at any one time for economic growth and social justice and the needs of the individual for personal development and fulfilment. In education, there is a depressing tendency for problems and recommended solutions to reappear over time like old films. This year's fashion is likely to be branded next year's misjudgement, and this year's cure-all will doubtless be identified as the prime cause of next year's difficulties. In such circumstances, detailed prescription from the centre (particularly if it is motivated at least in part by political conviction and liable to change as the balance of political power changes) may well prove to be mistaken, confusing and counterproductive. Real progress in the longer run is more likely to come from a variety of different educational approaches and initiatives at local authority, institutional and individual levels. This is essentially what Jones and Stewart[11] call 'advance from diversity and difference' or, put another way, it is the 'bottom-up' model of educational progress which Kogan[12] describes and endorses.

The fourth argument is to do with the 'mediating role' that local authorities, along with other organisations and groups in society, ought to perform in interpreting central government policies sensibly and sensitively to the consumers of public services. In education (and in related services like social welfare – and health), decisions about policies, priorities and methods and standards of service provision bear very directly on the everyday lives of ordinary people. And therefore as many decisions as possible, within a broad national framework, should be taken as far down the line as possible by bodies whose members are close to the people who actually use the services and are thoroughly aware of their needs, experiences and aspirations.

The fifth argument, closely related to but distinct from the fourth, concerns the differences between localities and the diversity of local needs. Despite modern communications and the artificiality of some of the present local government boundaries, there are very great (some would say rapidly increasing) differences between different parts of the country and between individual communities within the same part of the country. Some of these differences may be the recent 'artificial' outcomes of arbitrary external factors like government economic and financial policies, but many have their origins deep in the past and yet remain peculiarly powerful and pervasive in the present. These latter differences, in relation to a service like education, manifest themselves in a whole variety of ways, some of them obvious and on the surface, some of them subtle and deep-rooted. Members and officers of elected local authorities, it is argued, come to know about these things almost instinctively; they are well placed to harness local energy and pride, to know how best to implement national policies in accordance with local needs and circumstances, and to respond effectively to local enthusiasms and clearly expressed local preferences. This should make for a much richer, warmer and livelier service with much more consumer satisfaction than could ever be achieved by uniform central government directives painstakingly and unimaginatively implemented by locally based civil servants.

The sixth argument is, perhaps, the most difficult and certainly for the education service the most important. It is concerned with the morale of the education work force, particularly the professional teachers, and specifically those who are actually teaching in the schools and in further, higher or continuing education, as opposed to adminstering or advising or training or supporting or whatever. For it is on the competence, confidence, commitment and morale of the practising teachers in their day-to-day, face-to-face contact with their students that the success or failure of the whole elaborate structure ultimately depends. And it is only through the goodwill and cooperation of the practising teachers that beneficial changes of lasting significance can be achieved in the education service. Central government, it is argued, has not in recent years, despite its constant and wholly laudable concern to improve the quality of educational provision, been conspicuously successful in raising, or even sustaining teacher morale. In such circumstances, local education authorities can, if their own attitudes are right, at the very least act as a buffer and at best take very positive steps to support and ultimately restore the morale of 'their' teachers in ways which would not be open to or would not appear convincing from local officers of central government.

These arguments taken together provide a very formidable case for some form of democratic local control over the education service. However, they do not of themselves point to one particular form of local government nor could they properly be adduced in support of an established system of local government which was in practice failing to fulfil the purposes implicit in the arguments and failing to respond effectively to the needs of the times. Local government is neither self-justifying nor self-perpetuating; it has no right to survive regardless of how it performs.

The LEAs and the partnership

Prior to 1944, the public education service could hardly be described as a coherent national system. Indeed there was some justification for Tyrrell Burgess's verdict[13] that before 1944 English education was 'the result of a haphazard accumulation of inadequacies over the centuries'. But the great 1944 Education Act changed all that. Conceived in the dark days of war, it was a splendid expression of the nation's faith in its own and its children's future. Though much amended by subsequent legislation, it has remained ever since the statutory basis of our education system. It confirmed the multi-purpose counties and county boroughs as the local education authorities (the old Part III Authorities responsible for elementary education in some urban areas under the 1902 Act ceased to exist, though arrangements were made, and continued till 1974, for 'divisional executives' and 'excepted districts' to exercise certain delegated powers). The Act also laid down the ground rules for the 'partnership' which has been at the heart of our educational system ever since and which in the view of many people was until recently a prime source of its strength. That partnership – between central government, local government and educational institutions; between statutory and voluntary agencies; between professionals, parents and communities; between teacher and taught – now seems increasingly fragile and in danger of breakdown, but it demonstrated a remarkable degree of strength and resilience for the greater part of the postwar period. It was, and is, a partnership which depends as much on custom and convention as on law. It involves a division of powers with responsibilities held and responsibilities passed on at each level, but it involves much more than that. Partnership also implies recognition of and commitment to a common purpose, mutual confidence and respect, and above all (as Lord Alexander emphasised many years ago), 'continual cooperation at all levels'. And it implies a genuine effort by all concerned to understand the real nature and delicacy of the partnership, and to respect both its letter and its spirit.

The terms of the partnership, as defined by the 1985 SEO President,[14] were that

> the Minister determined national policy and the allocation of resources; the LEA implemented national policy with a substantial local discretion; and the individual establishment was responsible for the curriculum and how it was taught . . . The teachers' associations, although not legal partners, were assiduously consulted and in practice had almost partnership status. The churches, despite some initial reservations, found that cooperation with the LEAs under the 1944 settlement worked reasonably well. The parents were legal partners, but their terms were compliance.

Many writers have commented at length on the nature of the partnership, and in particular on the changes of emphasis within the partnership according, for example, to whether national government objectives for education were 'hard' or 'soft' and whether the local education authorities did or did not speak and act effectively together. One point is perhaps of special significance here. Whatever view may be taken of the 'independent' moral or historical legitimacy of democratic local authorities as such, there can be no doubt that the education partnership of the 1944 Act was not and is not in any meaningful sense a partnership between equals. The United Kingdom, despite the apparent contradiction involved in having separate systems of public education for England and Wales, for Scotland and for Northern Ireland, regulated by separate Acts of Parliament, is essentially a unitary not a federal state. The Queen in Parliament is the sovereign authority and the Secretary of State as the Queen's minister does have a clear duty under Section 1 of the 1944 Education Act to 'promote' the education of the people of England and Wales and to 'secure the effective execution by local authorities, under his control and direction, of the national policy for providing a varied and comprehensive service in every area'. That duty, which must be exercised in accordance with the law, is backed by powers of direction and intervention under Sections 68 and 99 of the Act if a local education authority is acting unreasonably or is in default. The LEAs have an equally clear duty under the same act to contribute 'so far as their powers extend' towards the spiritual, moral, mental and physical development of the community by securing that efficient education in three progressive stages (primary, secondary and further) is available to meet the needs of the population of their areas. It serves no purpose to argue as if those statements were not part of the law or did not mean what they say. As Alan Alexander [15] and many others have emphasised, local government in constitutional and financial terms is 'a subordinate form of government'. Local education authorities (as the 1976 Tameside judgement showed) have a right to determine their own educational policies within the law, and are not subject to the arbitrary whim of government ministers or officials, but they have no independent right to create law or to operate outside the law. Their functions are limited to those areas in which the law gives them a duty or a power to act. In somewhat similar ways, the duties, rights and responsibilities of governors and heads of institutions, and of parents and students, are defined by the law or by statutory regulations and articles of government made under the law. These arrangements, though traditionally held to be baffling to foreign visitors, have been well enough understood by those involved over forty years and would not perhaps be worth re-stating now were it not for the fact that in recent years some local authority voices have appeared to be claiming the right not only to criticise central government and even frustrate its intentions within the law but also to act outside the law by reference to a higher morality or their commitment to a separate 'mandate' obtained from the local electorate. Local government must accept that it is a subordinate and local form of government, and if it does not like its current relationship with, or the policies and practices of central government, it must endeavour to persuade central government to change the law and/or its policies and practices by rational argument and by demonstrating that it has strong popular support. It will clearly be easier for local government to influence central government if it is able to speak with a united voice about local government issues with the support of its workforce and its local communities. And equally clearly it will be hard for local government to secure any changes of long-term benefit from central government if it is seen to be riven by party political divisions and largely preoccupied with issues which seem of small significance to the providers and users of the services for which it has responsibility. It is all too easy for the centre to divide and rule in such circumstances, and one of the most important lessons that local government has to relearn in relation to education is that it cannot contribute effectively to the national education partnership if it cannot achieve partnership within its own ranks.

It is clearly wrong for local authorities to act or threaten to act outside the law and it is wrong for them on doctrinaire political grounds to withhold the day-to-day cooperation with central government on which the efficient administration of existing local services depends. But it is equally wrong, and far more damaging in the long run, for central government to abuse its power by exploiting to the limit the letter of the law and ignoring its spirit. It has long been accepted that in the United Kingdom the conventions of the constitution are in many ways as important as the law itself, and it is certainly true that laws, however carefully made, do not implement themselves and may have few positive effects, or even totally unintended outcomes, unless they are interpreted at the 'implementation level' with intelligence, skill, sensitivity and enthusiasm. And more than that, it would surely be unreasonable of central government to create or sustain a system of local government unless it intended the local authorities to have sufficient powers, resources and discretion to justify their existence. There is no point in maintaining systems and institutions unless they have the means of fulfilling their essential purposes.

The interest of local education authorities in maintaining an effective partnership is not confined to the central/local relationship nor yet to the relationship between those who manage, those who provide and those who use the service at local level. Because education has since 1944, indeed since 1902, been one function (albeit far and away the largest and most costly) of multi-purpose local authorities, there has also been a need to develop and maintain effective and harmonious working relationships with other committees and departments of the local authority and with the local council as a whole. Here again, the tensions and strains (never wholly absent) have become increasingly severe in some areas in recent years, particularly in those areas where extreme interpretations of 'corporate management' theory have been rigorously applied. The need for, and benefits of, cooperation between the education service and departments providing legal, financial, architectural and similar services for the whole authority are somewhat different in kind from those between education and other 'service' committees and departments like social welfare, community health (up to 1974) or police. But the value of cooperation, wherever it can improve services for the benefit of the community or help to resolve problems, is self-evident. Such cooperation has not always been all that it might have been in the past (and, it must be said, the fault has on occasions lain as much within education committees and departments as outside) but in some authorities over substantial periods of time it has been very good indeed. Similarly, and inevitably, there have been wide differences between authorities and over the years in the warmth and effectiveness of the relationship between the local authority elected members, the officers, and the teachers and other professionals in the field. Here again, despite some bad cases, there have been many examples of mutual respect and esteem proudly acknowledged by all concerned, and more than a few cases of inspired and inspiring leadership which produced remarkable results in circumstances which were often far from ideal.

Throughout the whole postwar period, every LEA was required by law to appoint an education committee with 'added members' representing educational interests and (except in cases of urgency) to receive a report from its education committee before taking decisions on matters affecting the education service. Apart from two reserved areas (raising loans and levying rates) the LEA could at its discretion delegate all its educational functions to its education committee. Each LEA also had by law to appoint a suitable person as chief education officer. Both requirements – a statutory education committee and a statutory education officer – were hotly contested by the local government 'corporate' lobby in the debates preceding the 1972 Local Government Act, and only retained after a considerable struggle.

Education was always the biggest service and the biggest spender in local government and for some twenty-five years after 1944 it was, despite numerous falterings and setbacks, growing and developing at a remarkable rate. In many authorities the education committee and the education officer enjoyed a substantial degree of autonomy and considerable prestige. For these and other reasons, the education committee usually attracted to its membership a substantial proportion of the most senior and influential aldermen and councillors in the authority. The chairmanship of the education committee was recognised as one of the most important jobs within the authority, offering not only great power and influence in the locality but also direct access to national influence via the Association of Education Committees and the education committees of the County Councils Association and the Association of Municipal Corporations.

However, even before 1974, the strength of the education committee was not always as unassailable as it appeared. It had in the last resort no real financial independence within local government and this fact was underlined when central government's specific grants for education, operative since 1902, were merged into the general local government grant in 1958, although the adverse consequences for education were largely concealed as long as economic prosperity and expansion continued. The statutory position, prestige and sometimes deliberate isolation of the education committee gave rise to criticisms and jealousies in other committees and departments of the authority. The education committee also was specially vulnerable to the growing party politicisation of local government. The cities and boroughs had always been more party political than the counties, but until the later 1960s there remained large areas of common ground in relation to education and even in the most 'political' cities the majority party leaders and caucuses were usually careful to preserve at least the appearance of real decision-making through the recognised committee and council procedures. Again, in the 1950s and 1960s, the basis of local support for the education committee and the education service was often passive acquiescence in a system which seemed to offer reasonable standards, improved facilities and widening opportunities rather than positive enthusiasm and involvement, and education officers often felt that the need was to stir up rather than damp down public interest, criticism and demand.

'The Partnership Years'

Despite all the inevitable and avoidable stresses, weaknesses and failures of the system, and the unpromising base from which it had to start, the achievements of what have been called the 'partnership years' (roughly the quarter of a century following the end of the 1939–45 war) were formidable indeed. They provide a main theme of the earlier chapters of this book, and in recent years have figured largely in the inaugural addresses of several SEO presidents (e.g. Sir Roy Harding in 1977, Jackson Hall in 1985). They fully justify the comment by Harry Judge[16] that 'anyone who denied that substantial and permanent progress had been made in the generation since 1944 would invite and deserve ridicule'.

The basic facts are impressive enough. Between 1950 and 1975:

— the number of pupils in maintained and assisted schools in England and Wales increased from under six million to over nine million;
— some seven million new primary and secondary school places were built;
— the number of students in further education nearly trebled, in initial teacher training quadrupled and in adult education doubled;
— the number of candidates entered for GCE '0' level (which replaced the old School Certificate) increased nearly ten-fold and for 'A' level more than eightfold;
— the number of special schools and pupils in special schools increased three-fold, while the number of special school teachers increased five-fold;
— the number of students in public sector higher education institutions (i.e. excluding the universities and teacher training establishments) increased by a factor of something like seventeen;
— and total public expenditure on education as a percentage of total national income more than doubled and overtook defence expenditure.

However, even these facts do less than justice to the effort and commitment involved. It was not just a matter of coping with the birth-rate bulges and the 1947 and 1973 raisings of the school leaving age but also of reorganising the all-age schools to achieve 'secondary education for all' and before that was even completed reorganising secondary education all over again in most areas on comprehensive lines. There were also the problems of new school provision to cope with massive new housing developments, and the contrasting problems of inner city and rural depopulation requiring their own reorganisation and closure programmes. There was in many areas a chronic shortage of teachers accompanied by high staff turnover. There were formidable development programmes across the whole field of further and higher education and a lot of effort too was devoted to improving the range of and facilities for special education, the youth service, adult and community education, libraries and so on. In such circumstances, it was inevitable that the minds of many of the political and professional leaders in central and local government were heavily preoccupied with the quantitative aspects of educational provision, but it is a gross distortion of the truth to suggest that there was not also great concern for the qualitative aspects. The establishment of the Schools Council for Curriculum and Examinations in 1964 was a symbol of that concern, and although its subsequent history and eventual abrupt demise in 1984 may be seen as an expression of the weaknesses as well as the strengths of the partnership system, it did do a lot of valuable innovative work and inspired or encouraged a lot more. It remains to be seen whether the latest, more centralist initiatives in establishing new separate bodies for examinations and curricula will do better!

In the context of the 'partnership years', the role of the Minister (from 1964 the Secretary of State) was generally seen as having more to do with leadership and influence, resource allocation and priorities, than with detailed prescription. 'Good' Ministers, at any rate in the eyes of LEA members and officers, were those who respected the partnership and the 'consensus' approach, obtained a fair (or better) share of resources, and exercised strong and positive leadership. David Eccles, Edward Boyle and Anthony Crosland were in their different ways outstanding in these respects.[17]

Whether or not, as Ranson[18] has argued, there was a significant shift in the balance of power in relation to education during the late 'fifties and early 'sixties from central government to the LEAs, it is certainly true that there was 'enormous scope for LEA autonomy and discretion'. But that autonomy and discretion could only be exercised successfully in a favourable climate. It required strong and sympathetic Ministers at the top; broad agreement at national level between the DES, the local authority associations and the teacher unions (of the kind achieved for example in the 'Eccles, Alexander, Gould' periods in the 'fifties and early 'sixties); and real commitment to education at LEA level.

The working of the partnership in one important area – school building development – has been briefly described earlier in this book and at greater length by Stuart Maclure[19] whose skilful and sympathetic analysis prompted a *Times* reviewer to describe the period covered (1945 to 1973) as 'a golden age of successful cooperation' and to draw a sharp contrast between the optimism of those years and the current 'pessimism masquerading under the polite name of realism'. Surely, Derek Morrell of the DES back in 1961 was right to stress 'the excellent results that can be obtained when both sides regard their contribution as complementary one to the other' and – as Morrell would have been the first to agree – that judgement applies not just to school building but to all education.

Cracks in the System

There are various views about exactly when the balance of power within the education partnership began to shift significantly to the centre and away from the LEAs. Some would argue that as far back as 1958 the abolition of central government's specific percentage grant for education in favour of a block grant for local government services as a whole (or at least most of them) planted a time-bomb in the system which was bound to explode when the going got rough. The block grant system (replaced by 'Rate Support Grant' from 1967) was introduced by Macmillan's Conservative government at the instigation of the Treasury and welcomed by many local government voices outside education. However, from education's point of view, it had three fundamental weaknesses which became all too apparent later on: it deprived central government (specifically the DES) of an acceptable and reasonably effective means of influencing and to some extent controlling LEA expenditure and standards of provision; it made it easy for central government to indulge in the 'transfer of blame' syndrome – initiating new, and politically popular, policies and raising public expectations without providing the necessary resources and then blaming the LEAs for any shortcomings in performance; and it reduced the status and undermined the special position of the education service within local government.

There are others who see 1965 as the critical turning point for education, and argue that 'in retrospect, the end of the freedom of LEAs to push ahead with their own policies was signalled by Circular 10/65, despite its lack of bite'.[20] Certainly, for many education officers Circular 10/65 (and Circular 10/66 which increased the pressure on LEAs) marked the beginning of the end of national and local government consensus on education as Wilson's first Labour government began to push all LEAs, whether they and their local communities wanted it or not, down the politically controversial road of comprehensive secondary schooling. Before long the Labour government was contemplating legislation to force all LEAs to toe the comprehensive line and in 1976 actually passed an Act to that effect – but that Act was promptly repealed by Mrs Thatcher's government which came to power in 1979, just as Circular 10/65 had been withdrawn by Heath's Conservative government (with Mrs Thatcher as Secretary of State for Education and Science) in 1970. These and similar developments (like Labour's 1975 announcement of the end of the Direct Grant Grammar Schools and the 1980 Conservative scheme for assisted places in independent schools) increased the differences between Labour and Tory policy at national level and embroiled the education service more and more, to its great distress, in the machinations of 'conviction' or 'confrontation' politics which in the 1970s and 1980s all too often became the order of the day. Looking back, it seems very likely that more would have been achieved eventually in terms of the Labour government's own comprehensive reorganisation plans if it had not moved towards compulsion but had contented itself with encouraging LEAs along a road which many of them, including some Conservative authorities, were travelling anyhow. Certainly, the determination to push comprehensive reorganisation strongly from the centre as a kind of panacea whenever a Labour government was in power meant that inevitably the comprehensive principle became a matter of political controversy and that far too much time and energy were devoted to political argument and structural reorganisation of the secondary school system often to the neglect of the content and quality of what was going on inside it. And it is curiously ironic that when the Labour government lost office in 1979, it left the main centres of educational privilege, the independent schools, not merely intact but powerfully reinforced by many of the most prestigious of the former direct grant schools.

Both 1958 and 1965 were years of very great significance for education and local government but in neither was the full impact of the changes then begun immediately appreciated. The general mood of confidence and the belief in consensus and partnership continued, despite the alarm signals, through the 1960s and into the 1970s. The year that many, probably most, people in education felt was the definitive turning point was 1974. That year, following the international oil crisis and in Britain the miners' strike, the three-day week and the end of the Heath government, saw the beginnings of severe economic recession from which the country is still struggling painfully to emerge. It saw the early impact in the primary schools of falling rolls. And it saw the reorganisation of local government and the health services in England and Wales. Again the full effects were not perhaps all immediately apparent but the passing years served only to underline the significance of the changes and there is no doubt that for many LEA members and officers – and many teachers – things never felt quite the same after 1974. Recession, contraction and reorganisation were the key elements in a new set of circumstances which opened the way for the growth of centralism.

Looking more closely at the causes of that growth, it is an obvious but nonetheless important point that political, social, economic and technological developments have in the last few decades dramatically increased the pressure towards central control in all public services (including education) and in other aspects of our national life. In many ways, local government no longer appears as a 'natural' and necessary element in the political and social structure, and therefore its future preservation and development will require a much clearer perception of its values and a much greater effort of will than ever before. Britain is a small country with a large population. It has good communications and, for the most part, especially among the professional and technically qualified, a mobile labour force. Local government boundaries and loyalties are not always clearly defined. People see education as a general good and entitlement; they are more conscious of their rights than ever before, and are much more aware of how best to secure them through what Dudley Fiske[21] called 'the orchestration of consumer voices'. Almost all significant local activities and interests look in one way or another for national representation as a means of increasing their influence over central government. Central government in turn can and does appeal directly through the media to the people as a whole, and its management of the national economy, successful or otherwise, directly affects the security and well-being of virtually every citizen, while its ordering of priorities and commitment of resources provide or deny opportunity and support. In such circumstances, it is only to be expected, and it is not at all improper, that central government should be active in what have been identified[22] as the three key fields of macro-economic management, the promotion of national strategies and the prescription of minimum standards. As John Tomlinson[23] has observed, in relation to education:

> There can be no doubt of the need for a strong involvement by central government. At crucial stages in the development of the service, the centre has given a lead and it should be no surprise that a generation after the 1944 Education Act the centre is again active.

There are increasingly powerful arguments – educational and social, as well as political, economic and financial – for central government to become more active in areas of the education service which it has previously left alone. And for local government there is always a balance to be struck between acceptance of the proper role of central government and resistance to excessive interference. The question is not whether central government should have an important, even an increasing, part to play in the education partnership but whether it plays that part in such a way as to secure and reinforce the best contributions of the other partners or to reduce them to frustrated and resentful local agents of a national *diktat*.

All the tensions and difficulties might have been more effectively resolved if local government had not been relatively so weak and divided within itself and so unsure in the years surrounding local government reorganisation whether education was its 'jewel in the crown' or its 'cuckoo in the nest'. Looking back from more than a decade afterwards, it seems clear that reorganisation not only failed in its declared intention of strengthening local government but also positively added to the problems and accentuated the weaknesses and divisions. Alan Alexander[24] identified four 'central principles' which were held at the time to justify the reorganisation and by which its subsequent success should be judged – 'efficiency, comprehensibility, local autonomy and conclusiveness' – and concludes that on all four counts the 1974/5 reorganisation was a failure, though less obviously in Scotland than in England and Wales. The reason for that failure was not that the Royal Commission on Local Government got it all wrong. The Redcliffe-Maud report (1969)[25], though criticised in detail by educationalists (e.g. as to the minimum desirable size of authority and the arrangements for local community involvement), was generally welcomed by them as a perceptive analysis of the main weaknesses of local government and of the reforms needed to correct them. But in fact the reorganisation finally embodied in the Heath government's 1972 Act was a shabby, botched-up political compromise which ignored or flouted virtually every one of the Redcliffe-Maud principles and which uncharitable minds might justifiably have condemned as a deliberate plan even then to keep local government weak and open to increasingly detailed direction from the centre. The Act did not create the unitary, multi-purpose local authorities which Maud (outside the three largest provincial conurbations) had strongly recommended, but rather preserved, indeed extended, the two-tier system with division of function. It did not (as the Seebohm Committee report on Social Services[26] had also strongly recommended) unite the Education, Social Services, Public Health and Housing functions at the same level of local government to facilitate cooperation, but instead split the housing function off in the shire counties and (by a separate Act of Parliament) took the school and community health services out of local government altogether. It did not make all LEAs large, powerful and reasonably equal, and therefore left central government well placed to play the 'least common denominator' line whenever it seemed advantageous to do so. It did not in some cases create the best balance between town and country, industry and agriculture (even where it would have been relatively easy to do so). It did not pay overmuch regard to traditional loyalties or existing good going concerns. It did not create a more equitable, flexible and bouyant system of local government finance, nor in fact has any government since, despite another major report – from the Layfield Committee – in 1976[27], and a great deal of huffing and puffing in Westminster and Whitehall.

The 1974 reorganisation was in many ways 'the wrong reorganisation at the wrong time'. Its impact on individual LEAs varied enormously – for some marginal, for others traumatic. It had its enthusiastic supporters, but many people at the time, and more and more with hindsight since, saw it as a sadly missed opportunity. Few national politicians now go out of their way to remind the electorate of their responsibility for it, but it is interesting to recall that, apart from Prime Minister Heath himself, the principal responsible Ministers were Walker and Heseltine (Environment), Joseph (Heath) and Mrs Thatcher (Education).

Yet, for the education service, even the 1974 reorganisation, bad as it was, might not have seemed so difficult and unacceptable had it not been for three other sets of factors: the economic crisis of 1973–74 and the recession which has persisted in varying forms ever since; the increasingly adverse effects of party politics and 'corporate management' within local government; and the increasing vulnerability of the education service itself to internal and external pressures in a period of retrenchment and contraction.

It was a peculiar irony that by the time that the Conservative government's scheme for local government reorganisation actually came into operation, a Labour government, which would have produced a quite different scheme, had come into power at Westminster. And it was also ironical that it was the Labour government of 1974–79 which was forced by economic crisis and the threat of apparently uncontrollable inflation to set in motion the process of squeezing public expenditure on local authority services and thus effectively to deny to local authorities the resources that were really necessary to make reorganisation acceptable. Growth prospects were sharply cut back during this period, but relationships between central and local government remained on the whole amicable and there was no general sense of breakdown in the partnership. This was also the period during which the Consultative Council on Local Government Finance (established in 1975 to formalise earlier consultative arrangements between central and local government) appears to have been most effective and when local expenditure kept close to the guidelines.[28] Perhaps this was because, in spite of policy disagreements, the financial effects of the policies were usually agreed between central government and the local authority associations. It was not till 1979, when a Conservative government took office, pledged to remove unnecessary central controls and transfer as many decisions as possible from Whitehall to Town Hall, that local authorities really began to feel the increasing weight of centralism!

Within the local government world itself, the period surrounding reorganisation saw three very significant developments which were to make the education service feel increasingly uncomfortable about the local authority system as its proper and natural 'home'. The first of these was the intensification of party politics and the development of corporate management systems and attitudes at elected member level. The cities and boroughs (including the Inner London Education Authority and the London boroughs created in the reorganisation of 1965) were virtually all strongly party political anyhow, and from 1974 the non-metropolitan counties went overwhelmingly the same way. Moreover, the way in which party political control was exercised became more centralised, disciplined and ruthless. Although the Royal Commission had backed off a little from the recommendation of the first Maud report[29] that there should be in each local authority a very small central 'management board' (of five to nine members of the council) forming in effect the 'inner cabinet' of the authority and responsible for all key decisions, local authorities in 1974 almost unanimously followed the ideas of the Bains Committee (1972)[30] and developed systems which made their 'Policy and Resources' or equivalent committees of prime importance and at the same time restricted the powers and influence of the service committees. There was, as Alan Alexander[31] has observed, often 'an uncritical acceptance of the prescriptions of the Bains Report . . . frequently unaccompanied, especially in the shire counties and districts, by either a real understanding of the techniques, or an accurate perception of the political consequences implied by the new approach'. It is perhaps worth recalling that the Working Group of the Bains Committee, which was set up in 1971 jointly by the Environment Secretary and the local authority associations, was composed almost entirely, with one exception (and that not a local government officer) of local authority clerks and treasurers. But it was not so much the adoption as the perversion of Bains that really caused the trouble. And, more importantly still, behind the Policy and Resources Committees were the new-style or not-so-new party caucuses and party leaders. Increasingly key policy issues tended to be first discussed and key decisions taken, including major financial decisions, outside the normal committee procedures by party caucuses which in some cases were heavily influenced by people who were neither elected councillors nor appointed committee members. Thus committee debates often became merely a front for what had already been decided elsewhere by the party in power, often without the benefit of considered advice from the relevant professional officers. There was no longer a bench of aldermen (which had pre-1974 been in some respects the local equivalent of a House of Lords) to bring its experience and wisdom to bear and exercise some restraint upon the elected members. Many of the elected members themselves were either new to and totally inexperienced in local government or from a variety of not easily reconciled local government backgrounds. In many authorities the influence of members who knew and cared about education and put its interests before party politics was declining. All of this meant for the education committees that, although there was plenty of work still to be done, there was a growing sense of frustration particularly among more moderate members of the majority party, minority party and independent members, 'added' members and officers, that the clear intentions of the 1944 Act (confirmed in 1972) that all education policy issues should normally first be considered by the education committee were frequently not being observed in any but a purely technical sense. The education committee consequently lost status and prestige in many authorities, and its attractions for the most able and influential members became less. Some of the best transferred their main interests elsewhere within local government, some left local government altogether at the first opportunity. Whether, as some would affirm, the overall longer-term effect was a decline in 'member calibre' in local government generally is difficult to say[32] but certainly the education service as a whole felt itself threatened and damaged by these developments. Where there was strong, sympathetic and consistent political leadership within the council, the effects on education were not necessarily immediately apparent or severe, but where there was unsympathetic leadership, or frequent changes of political control or no real control at all, the effects could be almost disastrous.

The second development within local government which was often (though again to markedly different degrees in different authorities) very uncomfortable for the education service was the development of 'corporate management' at officer level. The concepts of cooperation, coordination and corporate planning were not new to local government, and many (though admittedly not all) chief education officers and their staffs had throughout the years of expansion cooperated willingly, harmoniously and on the whole effectively with other departments under the acknowledged, if usually fairly restrained, leadership of the clerk of the council. From 1974, a new style of 'corporate management' was introduced, based on ideas imported from (and already outdated in) the United States and expressed in the Bains Report. Encouraged by the Secretary of State for the Environment,[33] the new local authorities all appointed new-style 'Chief Executives', usually without departmental responsibilities, to act as heads of all the local authority services and activities, and to coordinate for greater effectiveness the work of all departments, usually through a chief officer 'management team' with a variety of substructures. Many of the chief executives were 'new men' since a large number of clerks, and other chief officers, of the former authorities retired at the time of re-organisation taking advantage of the very favourable early retirement terms then on offer. Most were former clerks or senior officers from clerks' departments with an occasional treasurer or planning officer. They took over at a very difficult time and it would have been surprising if they had succeeded in pleasing everyone in their new and complex roles. Some did a remarkably good job not only as leaders and coordinators but also as stout defenders of the services, but sadly, in respect of education, a substantial number were seen as anything but effective leaders and welcome allies. Some were felt to be too much the creatures of the political leadership and to have failed to reconcile their political with their managerial role; some were excessively interventionist; some appeared overly concerned with the mechanisms of management which they felt should be the same irrespective of the nature or needs of different services, and were either unaware of or unconcerned about the quality of service delivery and the problems of service departments. A recent American commentator[34] has identified the four main grievances of education against the 'Bains-style' corporate management as 'a perceived attempt to downgrade education in local government, more central control of authority decision-making, an insensitivity to the management problems of the service, and a deliberate reduction of financial support'. Certainly that was how it all looked in some authorities, and equally certainly some chief executives played a big part in making it look that way. And added to those grievances was a fifth: a huge waste of officer time in useless meetings and a massive diversion of energies from important to ritual and trivial tasks. A city chief education officer (Michael Harrison)[35] described 'the blight of Bains' as 'the really gratuitous time-waster' and deplored the 'short-sighted folly' which loaded outworn and ineffective management systems onto key services which needed to be driven hard in the national interest. Many education officers would share his view. The case for and against Bains-style corporate management and chief executives has been argued at length since 1972 and is still being argued. Nobody with local government experience would deny the need for corporate planning and interdepartmental cooperation or for a recognised chairman or leader of the chief officers of whatever central and service departments the authority includes. But whether that leader should be a 'chief executive' or more like an old-style 'clerk' or some other kind of *primus inter pares*; how far fruitful corporate activity can be taken in local government when the services for which it is responsible are so disparate and in some cases unrelated and when some of the services which are closely related are outside local government; how much time and resources should be spent on corporate as opposed to service activities by individual chief and senior officers and by the authority as a whole – these and many similar problems are still being worked out with varying degrees of success in different parts of the country. What is clear is that the new-style corporate management, in both its political and professional manifestations, when ineptly and insensitively applied, enormously added to rather than eased the very severe problems that the education service had to face in any case in the later 1970s and 1980s.

The third development which was very damaging for the education service was the abject failure of the English and Welsh local authorities, in contrast to their Scottish counterparts, to achieve a single national organisation to represent all their interests to central government from 1974 onwards, and the subsequent demise (or, as some would say, 'political assassination') of the AEC which, as the first half of this book clearly demonstrates, had very effectively provided in the postwar period up to 1974 the necessary single, national voice for the education interest. The failure to achieve a single local government association was no doubt made inevitable by the nature of the structure introduced in 1974[36], and it led directly, though it need not have done, to the end of the AEC. The circumstances which led to the AEC being forced to close down in 1977 are described earlier in this book; they were a combination of party politics, the local government 'corporate' lobby, and personal animosities and jealousies. The formation of the Council of Local Education Authorities in 1974, as a creature of the AMA and ACC reflecting their political differences, was a clear signal from the new Local Authority Associations that they wanted no more of a body which dared to speak independently at national level (often across party lines and always with members and officers together) for education as a local government service. Despite strong pleas from some education officers (e.g. the writer as SEO President at the second CLEA annual conference in Cardiff in 1975) the Local Authority Associations had their way. Thereafter, although valiant efforts were made by leading members and officers of the education committees of the ACC and AMA and of CLEA, the local authorities generally failed to present a united front and speak with a single voice for education to national government, just as they generally failed to present themselves nationally to the teachers as caring employers committed to the interests of the service or to take necessary new initiatives on a national scale and thus resist the centralist inroads from the DES and from that 'wealthy interloper', the Manpower Services Commission.

From the early 1970s, the education service itself came under an increasing barrage of criticism from many quarters. It was almost bound to do so as it became obvious that all was not well in post-imperial, post-industrial Britain, and more and more people felt increasingly insecure, anxious and guilty. After all, from 1944 the education service had aspired – overweeningly, no doubt – to contribute to the enrichment of every aspect of our national life 'from the cradle to the grave'. It had been expected 'to fuel economic growth, facilitate equality of opportunity and afford some social justice to the deprived' and 'to bring a new world out of the old'.[37] As with other aspects of the postwar welfare state, the hopes placed in education were extravagantly high, and the disappointment at the outcomes correspondingly great. For, as John Dewey pointed out many years ago, education does not merely create but also inevitably reflects social values. It was therefore peculiarly vulnerable to all the anti-authority, anti-discipline, permissive, self-indulgent, materialist pressures that developed at an increasing rate once postwar austerity was brought to an end. The nation that had 'never had it so good' was not disposed to give its wholehearted support to the values and standards that most educationalists still wanted to promote for all children. And within the education service itself, there was a wide and widening gulf between the conservative and progressive elements, the former conscious of their heritage and slow to change even when change was urgently needed, the latter eager for change but too often mistaking trendiness for real improvement and adopting a kind of false egalitarianism which led to an under-emphasis on quality and a sloppy, disorganised approach curtly dismissed by Sir Alec Clegg as 'like a wet playtime all day'. Most teachers, of course, were somewhere between the extremes, but public confidence was not enhanced by the noisy clamour of the extremists, and there was a growing feeling that as opportunities were being widened, so standards were being allowed to slip.

There is little doubt either that in some respects the expansion of the 1950s, 1960s andf early 1970s was over-rapid and inadequately controlled and disciplined, though this was by no means always the fault of the education service alone. For example, teacher recruitment and training in the years of staff shortages and 'quotas' were not always as rigorous as they might have been. Comprehensive secondary reorganisation schemes were sometimes badly planned, inadequately resourced and unnecessarily disruptive, but they were pushed through more for political than educational reasons. In some primary schools there was poor quality, unimaginative traditional work and in some others half-baked, progressive work – the very disturbing case of the William Tyndale school in Islington, which hit the news headlines in 1975–76, was grossly overplayed by the media but was sufficiently symptomatic of real problems elsewhere to cause wider concern. The criticisms of educational standards in the 'Black Papers' (1969–76) and in Rhodes-Boyson's *Crisis in Education* (1975)[38] were in some measure and in some places justified. The best was very good indeed but the rest was not always good enough and the differences between LEAs and local communities within LEAs were often very marked indeed. Moreover, the image of the teaching profession in the eyes of the general public was not enhanced by the increasing militancy of some of the teacher unions in relation to their frequently legitimate grievances about salary levels before and after the Houghton settlement of 1974.

The uncritically optimistic 'all we need is more of it' approach to education had begun to break down as disagreement grew over the pattern of provision, content and standards, and it collapsed once it became clear that educational and economic expansion were not as it were two faces of the same coin. When the decline in the birth rate which had begun in 1964 and continued till 1978, began to have a serious impact on the schools from the early 1970s, and to all the problems of recession, retrenchment, and reorganisation were added the management of contraction, the difficulties for education were formidable indeed. The service which was far and away the biggest spender in local government but which in reality had very little room for manoeuvre[39] now found itself deprived of its strongest arguments for preferential treatment and increasingly under attack from competing services with apparently stronger claims at both national and local levels. And there were many other new and savage pressures – the changing demands of industry (manifestly important but practically never clearly articulated by industry's own representative bodies); the problems of growing unemployment especially amongst the young and less well qualified; inner city deprivation and the decline of many of the old industrialised areas; ethnic minority needs; changing patterns of community and family life; violence and hooliganism; alcohol and drug abuse; and so on. On top of all these, quite a number of politicians together with a significant part of the press and broadcasting media, industrialists, parents and pressure groups, conveniently overlooking their own share of responsibility, found it useful or profitable or both to sensationalise the failures and occasional crises and to treat the education service and local government as scapegoats. So criticism mounted and the demand for increased central intervention and direction became more insistent with little effective response from the politically divided local authorities and their national associations. Nor was there much comfort to be drawn from the fact that other 'western' countries with different political systems and economic circumstances were going through very similar crises of confidence in their public education services.

The march of centralism

In the 'partnership years' before 1974 there grew up among local education officers a folk-lore which said that Labour governments were generous towards education and other welfare services but also interventionist and prescriptive in their relationships with local authorities, whereas Conservative governments were more parsimonious but also more inclined to tolerate, even encourage, local differences and to leave as much decision-making as possible to local authorities. Like all folk-lore, it had within it a substantial element of truth and it even found expression in party political manifestos at the time of parliamentary elections. But like most folk-lore, it was a very inadequate guide to the real thinking and actions of government, especially when the pressures built up. Certainly the history of recent years provides no justification whatever for the view that a predilection towards increasing central control over important public services is an attribute of one political party only. Nor is it only one party that has demonstrated a capacity to injure whilst professing to reform and strengthen, or that prefers pragmatism to principle when 'the chips are down'. It is therefore only mildly surprising that the 1979–85 Conservative government, whose rhetoric has always been about getting rid of restrictive central government controls and 'rolling back the frontiers of the

State' and whose economic policies are so much to do with local initiative, free enterprise and virile competitiveness, should have achieved the reputation of being the most centralist government of modern times in its relationships with the education service and local government. Different problems of course require different solutions and all governments must respond to situations as they develop and adjust their policies accordingly. Recent central government action has certainly in part been justified by the attitudes of some LEAs (either savage and unreasoning defiance or supine compliance according to local political circumstances) and, as the 1985 White Paper *Better Schools* argues, by the need for still higher standards in a competitive world and the disparities of provision, qualitatively as well as quantitatively, between LEAs. Many educationalists would readily acknowledge the need for some more and more effective central government intervention in a number of key areas of the service. Of course, as educationalists they are primarily concerned with the growth and development of individuals and with the reconciliation of differences, and to that extent are inevitably 'wet' and deeply suspicious of many aspects of the now fashionable 'macho' approach to politics with its seemingly endless confrontations. But that is not to argue against central government action where it is needed, for example, to promote new policy initiatives necessary in the national interest, to discipline irresponsible factional interests or to guarantee acceptable minimum standards. It is simply to say that the line between appropriate and excessive central government action is a thin one, and that the perceived purposes and spirit behind the actions are often as important as the actions themselves.

The 'levers of centralism' took many forms after 1979. The first and most potent instrument was financial, and here (as A Alexander[40], Judge[41], and others have pointed out) the continuities of central government policy across the general election of 1979 proved remarkably strong. It was the Labour government of 1974–79 that started to squeeze the annual Rate Support Grant settlements and to reduce the percentage of local government expenditure paid by central government grants. It was also the Labour government that cut capital building programmes and introduced 'cash limits' as well as joint circulars of guidance to accompany the Rate Support Grant settlements. The Conservative government from 1979 carried the process much further and faster. It set out not only to bring overall local government expenditure under strict control, punish overspending, reduce local discretion and eliminate waste, but also massively to shift the balance between central and local funding of local government services. In relation to education, it sought to achieve improvements through the redeployment or more effective use of existing resources and at the same time took steps to secure some elements of centrally controlled, earmarked ('specific') funding, and to feed money into central agencies rather than into local government. The percentage of overall relevant local government expenditure paid by central government which had risen to 66.5 per cent in 1975/76 dropped rapidly and continuously in the 1980s to 48.7 per cent in 1985/6 and only 47 per cent for 1986/7. One of the greater failures of local government public relations was its inability to convince the general public (despite confirmation from the Audit Commission[42]) that this by itself inevitably meant considerably reduced services or higher rates or both, because the local proportion of expenditure on the relevant items had to rise correspondingly from 33.5 per cent to 53 per cent. The Central Council on Local Government Finance, though clearly a potentially powerful instrument for strengthening the partnership, was increasingly seen to have a limited influence on central government and to be more a receiver than a genuine negotiator of the grant settlements. The new 'Block Grant' arrangements, introduced by the Local Government Planning and Land (No. 2) Act, 1980, meant that from 1981–82 central government itself assessed the amount of 'grant related expenditure (GRE)' which each authority should spend on its various services, how much it could reasonably be expected to raise through the rates and therefore what difference should be payable as grant. Thus, authorities were put under much greater pressure to spend as the government intended they should, and from 1981/2 to 1985/6 were made subject to increasingly severe financial penalties by way of grant reduction if they overspent on their targets. When a number of Labour-controlled local authorities, foolishly no doubt, refused to toe the government line, central government in 1984 pushed through its 'rate-capping' legislation, which in effect, for the first time since they were established, imposed restrictions on the right of local authorities to determine the level of local rates at their discretion subject only to their accountability to local electorates. Nor was this all. Despite the well publicised weaknesses of the rating system (underlined once again in the Scottish revaluations of 1985), central government continually postponed action on the thorny problems of rate reform. Moreover, in the annual grant settlements, central government quite deliberately set and paid grants on targets for wage and salary increases for teachers and other staff which they must have known could not possibly be agreed, and then left the local authorities as 'employers' to bear the brunt of staff discontent, public concern at the disruption of schools, and the subsequent reductions in services necessary to meet the extra costs of the increases finally negotiated. Nor did government hesitate to pass legislation (like the 1981 Education Act on special educational needs) which raised public expectations and had clear resource implications for LEAs but for which the necessary additional resources were not made available. And when, in a significant move not otherwise entirely unwelcome to many education officers, the DES announced in 1983 a modest scheme of specific 'Education Support Grants' from 1985/86 through which central government would promote particular developments in the LEAs, it did so not by way of addition to but by deduction from the Block Grant. Thus, in every possible way financially, the LEAs were tied down and cut back. About the only significant additional freedom the LEAs acquired was the freedom under the 1980 Education Act to cut back on services which they had previously had a duty to provide, like school meals and milk and nursery education. In virtually every respect, except the scheme for assisted places in independent schools, the government's educational policy was 'conditioned by its overall desire to cut public spending'.[43]

The second great instrument of centralism was the Manpower Services Commission (MSC) which, despite the Conservative government's commitment in 1979 to get rid of as many 'quangos' as possible, became 'the biggest quango of all in the 1980s'.[44] Established in 1974 under the 1973 Employment and Training Act, the MSC, despite the opposition of Shirley Williams as Labour's Secretary of State for Education, was placed under the Department of Employment and, with a very wide-ranging brief, quickly acquired responsibility for a variety of work preparation, experience and training schemes, including special programmes for the young unemployed, as well as the more traditional employment services. Generously funded and with most of its key appointments made by central government, it became the chosen instrument through which government sought to grapple with the growing problems of massive youth unemployment. By 1983, when various smaller schemes including the Youth Opportunities Programme were brought together in the grand strategy of the Youth Training Scheme (YTS) the MSC was offering something like 350,000 one-year training places for unemployed school leavers at an annual cost of approximately £1,000 million, and from 1986 it will offer to all 16+ school leavers up to two years training, adding something like a further £1,000 million to the cost. The YTS is run through the collaborative efforts of industry and commerce, local authorities, voluntary bodies and consortia of various kinds operating under the control of Area Manpower Boards. Much of the off-the-job training and further education have been and will be of necessity organised and provided by further education institutions run by local education authorities, and MSC money has certainly helped to enable the further education system to respond more effectively than would otherwise have been the case to the obvious and urgent needs of the times. But there can be no doubt that central government action over the last decade and more in relation to the MSC has been a clear rejection of the former 'partnership' and a massive vote of no confidence in the ability of local government (and equally of the DES) to tackle the problems of youth unemployment and training swiftly and decisively. That is partly local government's own fault; in the early 1970s, preoccupied with other things, it showed no great capacity to generate the resolute, cooperative action needed to cope with the changing nature and scope of nation-wide problems, and its 'corporate lobby' exhibited an almost hysterical touchiness whenever central government specific funding of any major national initiative in education was discussed. But had local government been given the resources by central government, it might well have got its act together and achieved as good a response as the MSC or even possibly a better response because of its greater awareness of local needs and conditions. Who can tell? The fact is that from 1974, and even more from 1979, central government did not trust the LEAs to do what needed to be done.

Similarly, in relation to secondary education, the Conservative government clearly did not believe in the ability or the will of LEAs to promote in the schools the principles of utility and economic relevance on which it set so much store. The Technical and Vocational Education Initiative (TVEI) for fourteen to eighteen year old secondary school pupils announced in 1982 without any prior consultation with the LEAs, was 'a deliberate government action to use the MSC to intervene in the secondary school curriculum. . . . A well funded development was being offered on a pilot basis to an education service strapped for funds by a commission that was not accountable to the electorate nor in contact with the parents'.[45]

For the local authorities and their associations, it was humbling enough to have TVEI announced out of the blue as a *fait accompli* and then to have to go cap in hand to the MSC to ask for a share of the money. But even more humiliating was the *Training for Jobs* White Paper,[46] which in January, 1984, again without any prior consultation, announced that a substantial slice of the expenditure on work-related non-advanced further education previously under direct LEA control would in future be deducted from the grant settlement and added to that already being spent by the MSC on LEA-provided non-advanced further education. This would mean that in all about a quarter of all the money spent on work-related N.A.F.E. would be controlled directly by the MSC to be used as it deemed best, and not by the LEAs. The outcry from the local authority associations was immediate and – comparatively speaking – united and sustained. Eventually a compromise (the Nicholson-Harding plan) was worked out which provided for development programmes and plans for work-related non-advanced further education for each LEA to be drawn up in consultation with the MSC, employers and unions, and at national level an Advisory Group concerned with the whole of work-related N.A.F.E. So, the MSC, and by implication the government too, agreed in the event to continue to work in this area also in 'partnership' with the LEAs, and the latter were allowed to retain some shreds of their dignity – but the initiative, and at least *some* of the money, remained with the MSC. As the Audit Commission noted in its June 1985 report,[47] the whole affair was yet another development outside LEA control which 'made it increasingly difficult to manage the service at local level'.

All in all, the advent and development of the MSC radically altered the balance of power in education, and justified Harry Judge's verdict (1984)[48] that:

> most of the responsibility for the education and training of this (the sixteen to nineteen) group no longer lies with the educational agencies created in 1944 and redefined in 1974. It may be that, long before the end of this century, change on this scale will have the effect – desired or not – of terminating secondary education at the age of sixteen and of stimulating further the growth of a separate tertiary system, operating within different financial structures and under different control'.

Meanwhile, the LEAs had perforce to do whatever they could to establish and develop the most beneficial modes of cooperation.

The third area of vastly increased central government activity after 1979 was in relation to curriculum, assessment of standards, staff management and school government. Here again, the Conservative government, by a particularly 'hard' and aggressive interpretation of the so-called 'sleeping clauses' of the 1944 Act, exploited and intensified many of the things its predecessor had started. In terms of the curriculum, Prime Minister Callaghan's Ruskin College speech in October 1976 initiated the 'Great Debate' which brought to an end whatever was left of the 'secret garden' approach and led directly under the Labour government to DES Circular 14/77, seeking information on curricular policies from LEAs, and under the Conservatives to Circulars 6/81 and 8/83 requiring action by LEAs. At the same time there was a spate of guidance and discussion documents and reports from DES and HM Inspectorate, sufficient to promote from one chief education officer[49] the wry comment that from 1977 to 1985 'the HMI and DES between them published twice as much on the curriculum as they published previously in the years since the 1870 Education Act'. The White Paper *Better Schools* (March 1985) made clear that the aim was national agreement on the objectives and content of the school curriculum but that national syllabuses were not contemplated and that some diversity of interpretation at LEA and school level would still be regarded as acceptable and healthy. Also, in relation to the curriculum, the government in 1983–84 unceremoniously abolished the Schools Council and established two new bodies more to its liking – the Secondary Examinations Council and the Schools Curriculum Development Committee – to take its place. Moreover, the government set out to influence the curriculum both through TVEI and through Education Support Grants and to promote in-service teacher training through INSET grants, (soon to be extended by legislation) while it directed initial teacher training more closely through the new Council for the Accreditation of Teacher Education (CATE). In the field of public examinations, the government took decisive action to introduce the new GCSE examination on agreed subject criteria approved by the Secretary of State (to replace 'O' levels and CSE) in 1988, to add 'AS' to 'A' levels in 1989, and to develop pre-vocational examinations and records of achievement. It is also working, through the Secondary Examinations Council on Grade Related Criteria in the GCSE and through HMI and the Assessment of Performance Unit, towards national agreement on levels of attainment at various ages. With regard to staff management and appraisal, the LEAs had tried for many years to link salaries and conditions of service, either through the same Burnham mechanism or otherwise. Although they achieved this in further education, they could not achieve it also for school teachers because of the unwillingness of successive Secretaries of State to agree to the repeal of the Remuneration of Teachers Act. Only relatively late in the day did the DES seem to recognise the fundament problem which began to be highlighted in relation to midday supervision and other teacher activities at times of so-called 'industrial action'. Later too the government pressed the LEAs to introduce schemes for the regular and formal assessment of all teachers and, in the White Paper *Better Schools* announced its intention to legislate in order to give the Secretary of State power, in appropriate circumstances to require LEAs to appraise the performance of their teachers. On the government of schools, the 1980 Education Act guaranteed to parents more information, more choice and more involvement in the government of schools than ever before and *Better Schools* promised legislation to redefine and update the roles of LEAs, governors and head teachers (though not, as the Green Paper *Parental Influence at School* had proposed, to give parents a majority on the governing bodies of schools).

For most, if not all, the government's schemes and proposals on curriculum, standards and management, there was a powerful case to be made for strong action, and Sir Keith Joseph who became Secretary of State in 1981, must, whatever his shortcomings in terms of sensitivity and inspirational leadership, be given credit for genuine concern and the courage to grasp some pretty nasty and long-standing nettles. Individually, the various government initiatives were not easy to gainsay. Taken together, however, along with the financial constraints and the maraudings of the MSC, they all pointed in the same direction and did constitute a real threat. Nor is that the end of the story. In other areas too the levers of centralism were being forged. The University Grants Committee was becoming more and more the instrument of the government's relentless drive to achieve retrenchment, contraction and a shift in emphasis towards the vocational throughout the university system, while the National Advisory Board had the non-university higher education sector in what Tim Brighouse[50] called a 'vice-like grip'. The Audit Commission, another quango established in 1983, by transforming the old District Audit system into a new and more expensive form, harried the local authorities quietly but relentlessly in pursuit of the new 'managerial trinity'[51] of economy, efficiency and effectiveness. Even the heightened role of HMI noted by Harry Judge[52], though benevolent in most of its manifestations towards LEAs, must be seen as yet another centralist trend, particularly in view of the Secretary of State's intention announced in *Better Schools* to clarify the role of LEA advisers and make their work more effective.

Thus the Government established a host of commissions, councils, boards and committees to suit its purposes and strengthen its arm, while it got rid of those (like the Schools Council and the Advisory Committee on the Supply and Education of Teachers) which didn't fit in. Curiously, it conveniently 'forgot' its statutory duty under the 1944 Act to maintain a Central Advisory Council for Education, and almost equally curiously it consistently rejected over more than seven years repeated and urgent recommendations from the Warnock Committee (1978)[53] and later interested committees and organisations to establish a National Advisory Committee for Special Educational Needs. It did, however, in 1984 agree to one for Youth – and then for well over a year did nothing about setting it up!

The over-riding impression was of a government determined to have its own way, contemptuous of its 'partners', professing a determination to relax controls and decentralise decision-making but in reality doing the opposite, unwilling to listen to 'outside' independent expert advice. The whole style of government at senior civil servant as well as political level increasingly reflected those attitudes, and the total effect seemed quite clearly to be 'a conscious effort to subvert the institutional bases of our educational system . . . an assault upon autonomy and an attempt to accumulate all effective power in the hands of an aggressive central government'.[54]

References

1   Jones G W and Stewart J D: *The Case for Local Government* (Allen and Unwin, 1983) espec. p. 159.
2   Halsey A, Heath A and Ridge, J: *Origins and Destinations* (Clarendon Press, Oxford, 1980), p. 219.
3   Shipman M: *Education as a Public Service* (Harper and Row, 1984) p. 114 and p. 54.
4   Tomlinson J R G in *The Changing Government of Education*, ed. Ranson and Tomlinson (Allen and Unwin, forthcoming).

5   Jones G W and Stewart J D: op. cit., passim.
6   Alexander W P (now Lord): *Education in England* (Newnes Educational Publishing, 1954 – 2nd Edition, 1964), p. 2.
7   Shipman M: op. cit., p. 197.
8   Alexander A: *Local Government in Britain since Reorganisation* (Allen and Unwin, 1982), p. 171.
9   Shipman M: op. cit., pps. 117–8.
10   *Better Schools*: Government White Paper (Cmnd 9469) – official summary (1985) p. 2.
11   Jones G W and Stewart J D: op. cit., p. 75.
12   Kogan M: 'The Case of Education' in *National Interests and Local Government*, ed. K Young (Heinemann, 1983) pps. 73–74.
13   Burgess T: *A Guide to English Schools* (Pelican Books, 1964) p. 18.
14   Hall Jackson: SEO Presidential Address, Jan. 1985.
15   Alexander A: op. cit., p. 147.
16   Judge H: *A Generation of Schooling: English Secondary Schools since 1944* (Oxford, 1984) p. 212.
17   Gosden P: *The Education System since 1944* (Martin Robertson, Oxford, 1983) p. 19.
18   Ranson S: 'Changing Relations between Centre and Locality in Education' in *Local Government Studies* Vol. 6/6, 1980, pps. 7–10.
19   Maclure S: *Educational Development and School Building* (Longman, 1984).
20   Shipman M: op. cit., p. 53.
21   Fiske Dudley: SEO Presidential Address, January 1978.
22   Bush T: *Rhetoric and Reality – Relations between central government and local authorities* – SEO Occasional Paper No. 1 (1982), p. 4.
23   Tomlinson J R G., op. cit.
24   Alexander A: op. cit., p. 9.
25   Royal Commission on Local Government in England. Cmnd 4039, HMSO, 1969.
26   Report of the Committee on Local Authority and Allied Personal Social Services (the Seebohm Committee), Cmnd 3703, HMSO 1968.
27   Report of the Committee of Inquiry into Local Government Finance (the Layfield Committee), Cmnd 6453, HMSO 1976.
28   Crispin A et al: *Education and the New Block Grant*, London University Institute of Education, 1984, p. 22.
29   Committee on the Management of Local Government (Maud Report). HMSO, 1967.
30   Bains M A: *The New Local Authorities – Management and Structure* HMSO, 1972.
31   Alexander A: op. cit., p. 67.
32   Dearlove J: *The Reorganisation of British Local Government* (Cambridge, 1979) Cap. 8.
33   Alexander A: op. cit., p. 69.
34   Jennings R E: *Going corporate in Local Education Authorities* (Gower, 1985), p. 6.
35   Harrison G M A in *Education*, Vol. 165, No. 14, p. 303, April 1985.
36   Alexander A: op. cit., p. 152.

37 Ranson: op. cit., p. 3.
38 Boyson Rhodes: *Crisis in Education* (Woburn Press, 1975).
39 Shipman M: op. cit., Cap. 3.
40 Alexander A: op. cit., p. 166.
41 Judge H: op. cit., p. 184.
42 Audit Commission report on *The Impact on Local Authorities' Economy, Efficiency and Effectiveness of the Block Grant System*, HMSO, 1984.
43 Gosden P H J H: 'Education Policy 1979–84' in *The Conservative Government 1979–84* ed. D Bell, (Croom Helm, 1985), p. 105.
44 Shipman M: op. cit., p. 115.
45 Shipman M: op. cit., p. 117.
46 *Training for Jobs*, Government White Paper, Cmnd 9135, HMSO, 1984.
47 Audit Commission Report on *Obtaining Better Value From F E*, HMSO, 1985.
48 Judge H: op. cit., p. 195.
49 Brighouse T in *Education*, Vol. 165, No. 6., Feb. 1985, p. 128.
50 Brighouse T in *Education*, Vol. 165, No. 6., Feb. 1985, p. 128.
51 Hopkins K in *Education*, Vol. 165, No. 26, June 1985, p. 571.
52 Judge H: op. cit., p. 199.
53 Report of the Committee and Enquiry into the Education of Handicapped Children and Young People (the Warnock Committee) Cmnd 7212, HMSO, 1978.
54 Judge H: Article in *Times Educational Supplement*, 11.10.1985, p. 4.

Chapter 6

Future possibilities and needs

Future possibilities

The situation that now faces the education service within local government is, therefore, that all the apparatus for effective central government control is being assembled at an accelerating rate while local government remains relatively weak and disorganised, the education service (despite the many good features it undoubtedly still has) seriously demoralised, and the public largely indifferent except to excessive rate increases or manifest decline or disruption of services for which the local authorities always seem to take the blame. The news media and many politicians have clearly decided that education bashing and local government bashing have increasing popular appeal. True, there are some signs (autumn, 1985) that give grounds for hope. There is evidence, both at national and local levels, of a change in the political climate away from the extremes and towards a new consensus, but how significant and how lasting that will be remains to be seen. There is some evidence too that, under extreme pressure, the LEAs through their national organisations are sometimes beginning to come closer together and speak with a more united, local government voice. But the overall picture remains gloomy. And all those who are still determined to fight for local democracy should remember that in present circumstances virtually every argument for LEAs retaining a major responsibility for education can be stood on its head and used almost equally effectively in support of the opposite view. The bulwark of freedom argument does not seem so convincing to those who see in town or county hall local party political caucuses which are clearly undermining the open democratic processes and which as often as not were put into power by a minority of a largely apathetic electorate apparently only interested in national political and economic issues. The argument about counterbalancing excessive central power and providing for the practice of democracy sounds hollow when local leaders passionately demand their share of power from the centre but refuse to share it with their local communities and institutions. The efficiency and effectiveness argument loses its appeal when the main role of local government is retrenchment and contraction, and the necessary initiatives to cope with urgent new problems like massive youth unemployment are seen to be taken elsewhere. The argument about fruitful diversity is undermined if the most obvious feature of the LEA system is not health variety above an acceptable norm but increasingly unacceptable differences in standards of basic provision. Talk of mediating national policies and responding to local needs, circumstances and enthusiasms does not ring true if the local debate is little more than an echo of the national party political dogfight, and local priorities seem more concerned with political advantage, organisational systems and management than with local service provision. And the argument about protecting and sustaining the morale of the teaching force is a very uncertain weapon, far less reliable than a decade or so ago and deriving as much from the hostility (real or imagined) of central government to the education service as a whole as from any positive enthusiasm among the teachers for local government as such. In recent years it has not been helped by the ill-considered and intemperate action of a few LEAs which has positively contributed towards undermining teacher morale. The whole picture could well look very different if at some future date under a different government greater central control seemed likely to produce for the teachers greater appreciation, higher status, more generous resources and better conditions.

On the other hand, whilst it is certainly true that local government has contributed significantly by its own actions, and failures to act, to its present predicament, the case for major involvement of democratic local bodies of some kind in the control and management of the education service remains very strong. But it cannot be taken for granted and will not win the day eventually without very considerable effort from a lot of people in education, in local (and national) government and throughout the country.

The ways in which the present complex situation will evolve

during the rest of this century are extremely difficult to predict but there are certainly half a dozen possible lines of future development that the education service and local government ought to consider very seriously. Perhaps the greatest danger for local government in the years ahead would be to dismiss most of them as totally unrealistic. Fortunately, this is a good deal less likely than ten years back – not so many local leaders now have their heads in the sand, and only a few are unable, or unwilling, to see the storm clouds gathering.

The first alternative, which must be accepted at least as a theoretical possibility, is what may be called the 'change of heart' outcome. Assuming that the shifts in the political balance at national and local level continue, it is possible that this or some future government might take steps to re-establish and reinforce the education partnership concept broadly within the present constitutional framework and, hopefully with recovering economic strength, to create a new dynamic which would bring the currently conflicting interests into a more harmonious and productive relationship. It is also possible that the local authorities individually and collectively would take steps to put their own houses in order, re-affirm their primary commitment to local needs and service provision rather than national party politics, and move to more open and participative government through established committee and management systems with some modest changes designed to improve efficiency and re-establish confidence. There are certainly a number of 'good' LEAs who would have much less far to go than others in putting their individual houses in order and who would be able to influence national developments in the right direction. But this alternative, attractive as it sounds, would involve a very big and sustained change of heart by a lot of people over a long period. It would leave unresolved all the problems and tensions inherent in the present system. And it could hardly avoid being slow, uneven and uninspiring. It is very doubtful that it would command sufficient political and public support for long enough to succeed.

The second, and on the face of things, more likely alternative is 'creeping centralisation' – progressive takeover by central government within the existing system of all effective control of the education service with little resistance from the LEAs and at least the partial consent of a significant number of the education service professionals and consumers. The instruments for this kind of development are already to hand and further steps in the process are clearly envisaged. Reference was made to some of them in the previous chapter. Other possibilities which have already been discussed include:

- a central government takeover of direct responsibility for all teachers' salaries and service conditions, leaving the LEAs as mere agents rather than genuine employers;
- an 'education block grant', returning to something like the pre-1958 situation, which would certainly be welcome to some educationalists but would deeply offend many other local government interests;
- a significant change in government funding of local authorities generally which would make future rate support grant above a very basic level dependent on agreement in advance on the ways in which extra grants for exceptional needs would be spent.

'Creeping centralisation' would leave the form and appearance of things more or less intact but would steadily debilitate the local authorities, undermine their authority and destroy their credibility. It would virtually guarantee continuing central-local government conflict and at the same time progressively deprive the local authorities of the means of justifying their own existence by nourishing local initiatives and responding imaginatively in their own ways to the needs of their own populations.

The third, and again clearly possible alternative, is 'partial dismemberment'. The 'seamless robe' argument defended by many LEA educationalists since 1944 has never been particularly popular with some government ministers and officials (e.g. in relation to non-university higher education), and in recent years some LEAs have themselves done their best to destroy the argument by transferring parts of the education service (youth and community, adult, libraries, for example) to other departments like 'Leisure and Recreation'. But from the early 1980s the prime and obvious threat has been the Manpower Services Commission, so much so that in the summer of 1985 government ministers and headteachers in conference were openly talking, (though with very different levels of enthusiasm), of lowering the school leaving age to fourteen and transferring responsibility for all fourteen to nineteen education and training to the commission. Central government, so the argument runs, must respond more effectively to the acute public concern about massive and continuing youth unemployment and its related social problems. It is being reluctantly driven, because of the need to generate effective action quickly, to take over from the LEAs the education, training and counselling of all young people aged sixteen to nineteen, or better still fourteen to nineteen, or even perhaps, for ease of administration, eleven to nineteen. The Manpower Services Commission has of course already gone a good way in that direction, and clearly has ambitions to go further. If full takeover is eventually decided upon, the logic of the situation may well suggest that all LEA higher, further, secondary (post fourteen, probably), adult, youth and community provision should be taken over, combined with Youth Training and Employment services and run either directly by central government or through bodies which already exist (the UGC, NAB, CATE, NAG, MSC) or could easily be created. The local authorities would be left with the responsibility for running schools only for children up to the lower secondary stage but not beyond. That responsibility might (or might not) be left to multi-purpose local authorities but it would hardly justify the involvement of large county councils, and the county districts would not be slow to take up the challenge. The probable outcome would be an LEA schools service (not altogether unlike the old Part III authorities abolished in 1944) with responsibility at metropolitan district, non-metropolitan county district and London borough levels with a special arrangement for Inner London. That in turn might raise questions about where local responsibility for social welfare services should be located in future – and that just might (particularly if the political climate in Westminster was unfavourable to them) bring into question the continued existence of the shire county councils as such.

The fourth alternative is 'total takeover'. Substantial services (public utilities, water, community health) have been taken away from local authority control in the past and it is no longer wildly fantastic to suggest that in the fairly near future central government might quite explicitly and by Act of Parliament take over all the education services which are currently the responsibility of the LEAs and run them from the centre, possibly with some decentralisation of managerial and administrative functions to regional and local levels. After all, it is not clear that the more centralised education systems of continental Europe offer only disadvantages in comparison with our own, and, as has been argued earlier, the apparent attractions of greater central control in Britian have increased markedly in recent years. Moreover, there is the precedent of the National Health Service. When, under pressure from the medical profession, which reflected a long-standing hostility to and distrust of local government, the Heath government in 1973 rejected the idea of unifying the health services (hospital, general practitioner, school and community) within local government, and instead took what had been the local authority health services into an enlarged National Health Service operating through appointed regional and area (later district) boards, it struck a severe blow at the whole idea of local democratic control. For if the health services are outside local government, it is not immediately apparent why the education and social welfare services should be inside. And if education and social welfare were to leave local government, it would be reduced to such a minor role that the present elaborate system could not really be justified. It was this kind of consideration that led Lord Alexander a decade ago to say 'Education can do without local government but local government cannot do without education'. It will no doubt be argued now (as it was then) by local government leaders that any talk of total takeover of the education service by central government is thoroughly irresponsible and only serves to provoke ideas which didn't exist before. But the possibility is there, with a clear precedent. Whether the example of the National Health Service is one which the education service would wish to follow is another matter. And in any case it is not the only precedent. More to the point perhaps and in many ways more attractive for education officers and teachers is the example of Northern Ireland. In the 1973 reorganisation, the LEAs of Northern Ireland were replaced by five Education and Library Boards, each appointing their own staffs and broadly running their own services, but funded directly by the Northern Ireland Department of Education. The Boards are 60 per cent nominated by the Secretary of State, but his nominees must reflect church interests (25 per cent) and persons with knowledge and experience relevant to the education and library service (35 per cent). The remaining 40 per cent of board members are selected by the local councils from among their elected members. The Boards are generally not heavily political, and Northern Irish education officers are able to detect quite a number of advantages as well as some disadvantages in their present arrangements.

There are two other possibilities which need to be considered, both of which though in very different ways could serve effectively the interests of local democracy and the interests of the education service. Both would require a high degree of political and professional courage, commitment and perseverance because both would involve further major reorganisations. One of them, the fifth alternative, would require another reorganisation of the local government system. It would mean returning to the principles of the 1969 Royal Commission Report, reconstituting the existing counties, boroughs and districts into new unitary all-purpose authorities and restoring to them (within a freshly prescribed form of partnership between central government, local government, institutions, professionals and consumer/community interests) responsibility for all the 'cognate' public services which need to work together for maximum efficiency. What is envisaged here would be broadly, though not in every detail, in line with the radical reorganisation advocated by Jones and Stewart in 1983.[1] Specifically, it would mean that the new large unitary authorities (about one hundred in all in England and Wales with average populations round about half a million) would include education; health; social welfare; public protection (police, fire) and probation services; planning; housing management and development; libraries, museums and arts; amenities; leisure and recreation services. If all these services were brought together in this way, then the system of local government would really contribute towards rather than militate against effective inter-service cooperation, and enlightened corporate management would begin to make some kind of sense. This is what most LEA education officers would probably prefer. John Tomlinson has said recently, 'The paradigm is still Redcliffe-Maud's unitary, multi-purpose authorities'.[2] But the difficulties in the way of getting and keeping it right, particularly in relation to the effective subjugation of party political extremism in the interests of effective local service provision for local communities, would be formidable indeed. The vested interests are many and powerful, and another botched-up reorganisation would really spell disaster for local government.

If the fifth alternative were to prove impossible of achievement in any acceptable form, then in the view of a substantial and growing number of people including many who actually work in education, a sixth alternative (large, single-purpose, full-range, elected, rate-levying, local education 'boards') would be the best for the education service and the only one likely to rid education of the excesses of party political confrontation. There is a whole range of precedents and foreign examples to consider in this connection, though none provide a totally valid comparison with our own present circumstances. The school boards created by Forster's 1870

Education Act and the arguments which preceded their replacement by the multi-purpose local authorities in 1902 still have something to say. The present-day school boards of the United States and Canada seem increasingly attractive to English educators as their circumstances and *modus operandi* become better known and as the strains in our own system become increasingly apparent. For the most part in the States and generally in Canada, they are directly elected for education purposes only, have 'fiscal independence' under state or provincial law, receive additional monies from state/provincial and federal sources, employ their own staffs and are on the whole regarded by their officers as more education-oriented than party political in their approach and accountability. Although they vary enormously in size and have only limited responsibilities outside school education, they do exhibit a number of features which could well be worth our more serious attention, as well as some (e.g. in some parts of the States, the election of chief education officers) which we would surely find unacceptable. Then, turning back to the United Kingdom, we should not forget the thirty-eight *ad hoc* authorities which from 1919 to 1930 ran the Scottish counties and burghs. Elected by proportional representation every three years, the *ad hoc* authorities dealt with education only; their history and the circumstances of their passing provide an interesting case study,[3] and there are still Scottish educationists who talk of the period of the *ad hoc* authorities as a brief golden age of high calibre members, informed debates and freedom from political rancour. Then there is the Manx experience. From 1949 to 1968, the Isle of Man had a directly-elected rate-levying single-purpose education authority accountable in financial matters to a five-man committee of Tynwald, the Manx parliament; and since 1968, education has been run by a Board of Education of twenty-nine members (five including the chairman nominated by Tynwald, twenty-four directly elected every five years for education purposes only) with direct financing from the island's income tax. The island's director of education observed in 1979 (the millenial year of Tynwald) that the system ensures 'a prominent and special place for education in Island political life. It makes for open government and vests the members of the Board of Education with an authority which would surely be the envy of their counterparts serving on education committees in England and Wales'.[4] And he added later (1985)[5] 'Party politics do not play a significant part in the administration of education in the Isle of Man. Although it is technically possible for members to align themselves to a particular political party, this has not to my knowledge happened and all members are deemed to be independent.' There are many education officers, and education committee members too, in mainland Britain, who will read those comments with envy. And if it is objected that a small island offers no kind of realistic precedent for the much larger mainland authorities, then surely it must be significant that the present UK government has decided that, following the abolition of the Greater London Council and the six metropolitan counties in the spring of 1986, the education service in Inner London is to be the responsibility of a new directly-elected, rate-levying, single-purpose Inner London Education Authority. It is too early yet to say how clear a precedent the new ILEA will offer for the rest of the country, but it is good to note that parliament has removed from the abolition bill certain gratuitously offensive provisions which would have subjected the new ILEA in its early years to review and possible abolition by the Secretary of State, without further reference to Parliament.

Alternative five, if attainable in a relatively 'pure' form, could be good for education and good for local government but it is difficult to be confident that what proved impossible in the period 1969–1974 will somehow be agreed and implemented a few years from now. And it cannot be left too long! Local government is like any other seriously ill patient – if urgently needed treatment cannot be made available quickly or is deliberately withheld, it will become unnecessary because the patient will have died! Alternative six would undoubtedly be good for education but would create severe problems for the present pattern of local government. To have single-purpose elected local education authorities responsible for the full range of education but for education only, with clearly defined duties and powers, reasonable freedom of manoeuvre within a national system, and adequate discretion in matters of policy, practice and finance, would be very attractive for the education service. It should ensure high quality, interested, knowledgeable and committed elected members, a concentration on educational issues and educational arguments, and clear, unconfused lines of accountability to the local electorate. It should bring to an end for education, or at least reduce to more manageable proportions, the local party political excesses that have so disfigured the reputation of local government in recent years. But it would also at a stroke remove from the present multi-purpose local authorities which are LEAs one of their most important functions and more than half their staff and expenditure. So, it would be opposed – by a variety of powerful political and local interests, and it is for that reason that some commentators (e.g. Howell)[6] have dismissed it as 'politically quite unrealistic'. But the education service, with its half million teachers and millions of 'consumers', is a powerful lobby in its own right when it knows what it wants and speaks with one voice. It should not be assumed that what was unattainable will remain so if discontent with the present system increases and all other alternatives seem either unattainable or even more unattractive.

All the six alternatives discussed so far exclude the idea of a regional elected tier of government, and perhaps this should be added as a seventh alternative to be considered either separately from, or in combination with, some of the others. There has been quite a lot of political interest in recent years in the possibility of establishing elected regional councils which would take back from central government the services removed from local government in 1974 (i.e. health; water supply and distribution) and to which might be added certain other responsibilities, like higher education, public transport and utilities, police, strategic planning and emergency services. There are formidable arguments against regionalising any part of the education service, but the main objections are practical. There is little agreement in most cases at any rate, on regional boundaries and no obvious sense of regional loyalty.[7] It would be absurd for regional government to manage the day-to-day affairs of the 'personal' public services, and it would be equally absurd to have four major tiers of government in a small island – central, regional, county and district! That really would be bureaucracy gone mad! If regional government were ever introduced into England and Wales (the Scottish 'regions' created in 1975 are quite different), it would almost certainly mean the abolition of the shire county councils. That might happen – as an act of political revenge for the abolition of the GLC and metropolitan counties or as a result of the changes envisaged in some of the alternatives discussed earlier in this chapter. It would be bad for genuine local government and for education but it certainly cannot be ruled out as a possibility.

Future needs

There will no doubt be plenty of people in national and local politics, the news media and education itself who will argue that there are no problems in the present system that more money would not cure, that major structural changes are not required, and that the essential priority for education is the 'economic relevance' on which the present government lays so much stress. But economic relevance, though clearly a highly important consideration, is an insufficient vision for a worthwhile education service in a free, democratic society. True, the service is currently (1985) very short of funds and feeling the pinch badly (as the recent annual surveys by HM Inspectors of the effects of LEA expenditure policies have amply demonstrated). True, the service feels deeply affronted by the low status and inadequate share of available resources that have been accorded to it by the government and many LEAs since 1974. But more money alone (even lots more, which is hardly to be expected in the short term) would not by itself solve current problems and restore the situation. The education service must contribute to and share responsibility for the market economy and the consumer society, but it is concerned with values and standards and attitudes which go far beyond mere economic relevance and business success. It is concerned with nothing less than the quality of life of all the people. However pompous and pious it may sound, that is the simple truth. And if the education service is to contribute as it should and must to the future wellbeing of our troubled nation, it must feel secure within itself, confident of public support, and comfortable about the structures and systems within which it has to operate. At present, it feels none of these things, and despite many shining examples of high commitment and achievement, morale is deteriorating rapidly. If that is allowed to continue, the long term consequences could be too awful to contemplate.

What then are the fundamental priority needs of the education service for the rest of this century and beyond? I suggest there are five:

1 A new form of democratic control and accountability

Education is too wide-ranging in its impact and too 'political' to be left to the professionals. But it is also too important and too vulnerable to be forever at the mercy of the arbitrary, short term whims of party politicians at either central or local government level. The education service must, in our kind of society, be finally subject to the will of the people's representatives, but those who exercise the power nationally and locally should also have some knowledge and understanding, a measure of commitment which is more than career opportunism, and an awareness of their awesome responsibilities as well as their limitations. The system ought as far as possible to lead in that direction; in the view of many people, it no longer seems to do so. Moreover, if a reasonable degree of political consensus about educational policies is now to be regarded as unattainable, there must surely be some built-in guarantees of stability as well as provision for change and development. The service will never flourish if it is turned upside down every few years because party political dogma says it will work better on its head!

2 A new form of partnership

The essential message of the whole of this commentary so far has been that division of powers and partnership are essential to the health of the education service but that in recent years the partnership established by the 1944 Education Act has effectively broken down. There is a manifest need to redefine and restore the central/local government partnership and at the same time to reform and strengthen the local government component. There is also an urgent need (and not just in education) to clarify and improve the partnership between politicians and professional officers in central and local government. And there is a continuing need in education to promote a meaningful and fruitful partnership between professionals, voluntary organisations, parents, students and local communities.

3 A new form of teacher professionalism

Almost more than the LEAs, the teachers have suffered in their relations with central and local government, and in their 'image' and status in society, from the divisions and disagreements within their own ranks. There is a desperate need (surely demonstrated beyond doubt in the lamentable salary 'negotiations' and teachers' strikes of 1985) for them to achieve professional unity and play a much more decisive part as a profession in recruitment and training, professional appraisal and career development, professional conduct, educational policy formulation and development programmes.

4 A new form of leadership

Recent writers (notably Bush and Kogan, 1982)[8] have commented on the decline since 1974 in the power and influence of chief education officers. Whatever truth there may be in that (and, as always, the picture has varied enormously among LEAs), it is undeniable that the leadership role at central government level and in many LEAs is now in important respects more political than professional. And it is sad to record that in the education service there is a growing feeling that the political leaders at the very highest levels of central government and in a number of LEAs act as if they hold the service in contempt, do not know about or ignore its good points, are aware only of its faults and delight in publicising them. There is a great need for inspirational leadership at national and local levels to boost morale, restore confidence and offer hope and encouragement. The most disturbing feature of the present situation is that it is often the effective and committed teachers who feel most disillusioned. It is almost as if our political leaders, in circumstances not wholly dissimilar from 1939–1945, were trying to fight a war and calling for great effort and sacrifice without caring a damn for the morale of the fighting troops in the field!

5 A new synthesis of education and training

If the economic base required to sustain and improve the public education system and other related welfare services is to be effectively revitalised, there is an urgent need for a radical new approach to education and training as complementary aspects of a lifelong activity and entitlement for all, subject to the essential condition that all will be expected, and provided with the opportunities to contribute the best that they have to give to the community of which they form a part. This must mean a completely new bringing together of school, post-school and continuing education, training and re-training opportunities, work experience, community service and leisure activities, as well as employment policies and programmes. It must also surely mean the end of many outworn notions of status and class in our society, the removal of sources of division and discord, and the creation of a new sense of national pride and purpose, without which the economic miracle will either not be achievable or not worth achieving.

Even if the reality and urgency of these needs is accepted, there will inevitably be much argument about the strategies and mechanisms through which they might be met. It is my view that all the following will have to be considered:

A fundamental Bill of Rights

If in fact the divisions in our society deepen and politics become even more adversarial, there will very soon come a time when (in defiance of the British tradition) we ought to seek to agree – across party lines, before it is too late – a declaration of the fundamental rights and entitlements of individuals, a definition of the limitations of central power in relation to individuals, groups, and 'mediating' authorities/agencies, and a clear (or as clear as we can get) distinction between the 'state' and the government of the day.

A major reorganisation of local government

One major reorganisation of the systems of local government established in 1964 and 1974 has already been put into effect by the abolition of the Greater London Council and the six metropolitan counties. So – it can be done if the political motivation is strong enough! What is now needed is a further major reorganisation, inspired not by considerations of political advantage or retribution but by a genuine multi-party concern for the health of the education service and local government. Such a reorganisation would:

– create either unitary, multi-purpose, 'cognate' elected local authorities or single-purpose elected local education authorities;
– ensure that there was real and substantial local democratic control and accountability within a national system;
– provide the new authorities with adequate direct fund-raising powers at their discretion and assure them of appropriate central government financial support with equalisation arrangements to compensate areas of high need and low resources;
– ensure that the authorities were large enough to provide the appropriate range of services, reasonably equal, and embodied as far as possible real local traditions and loyalties;
– give to the authorities responsibility for the full range of educational provision across the age groups with adequate support services and covering both education and related training and community activities;

- safeguard the 'special position' of the education service and ensure that expert local education representatives and wider consumer/community interests were able to make a substantial contribution to the consideration of educational issues;
- ensure that the authorities were fully aware that their prime responsibility and only justification was the provision of high quality services in accordance with national policies and local needs, and that local political and management activity must be primarily directed towards that end.

A code of conduct

This should apply throughout local government (and there is strong evidence of a similar need in central government too). It might have to be imposed nationally by Act of Parliament but would preferably be achieved by voluntary agreement of all concerned through their national organisations and would regulate, in supplementation of the law, the proceedings, behaviour and relationship of and between elected members and professional officers. Its prime purpose would be to ensure that each side understood and respected the obligations and the legitimate rights and expectations of the other. Since 1974 education officers have been increasingly, sometimes painfully, aware of the need for such a code as the 'cult of the DEROPS' (the idea that the democratically elected representatives of the people automatically acquire knowledge, experience, judgement and management skills as well as power through the ballot box) has gathered force in some areas and as more elected members have felt it appropriate to take key decisions without relevant officer advice and even to involve themselves in the details of management. It was entirely right and necessary that the government in 1985 set up a Committee of Inquiry into the Conduct of Local Authority Business (the Widdicombe Committee) and the evidence submitted to that committee in July 1985 by the Society of Education Officers admirably summarises their beliefs and their concerns. It is very much to be hoped that one main outcome of this inquiry will be agreed codes of conduct and good practice to regulate 'relationships between the authority and its public, majority groups and minority groups and between officers and members' in order to create 'a climate of understanding and trust and acceptable behaviour'.[9]

A major new Education Act

There are conflicting views about whether a major new Education Act is now needed. Aldrich and Leighton[10] have posed the question again, and clearly their view is that a new act is needed. The education officer of the Association of County Councils[11] thinks the same because 'the 1944 Act (with all the subsequent mini-legislation) no longer provides an adequate basis'. The education officer of the Association of Metropolitan Authorities[12] thinks we do not need a new Act and that the 1944 'flagship' with its 'flotilla of smaller education statutes, responsive to change and not exclusively modelled on 1944 designs' will continue to serve well enough. My own strongly-held view is that a major new Education Act is needed, and needed urgently, in order to:

1 restate in current terms the aims and objectives of our national education service;

2 re-assert the principle of partnership in education and redefine the duties, powers and entitlements of the various members of the partnership (central government, local education authorities, institutions, voluntary bodies, teachers and their professional organisations, pupils, parents and the wider community);

3 provide for the creation of a new combined central government department under a Secretary of State for Education and Training;

4 provide in each LEA for a statutory Education Committee (of elected and 'added' members) with more clearly defined powers in the case of a multi-purpose LEA or prescribe procedures whereby a single-purpose LEA would have access to appropriate educational expertise other than its own members and officers;

5 provide in each LEA for a statutory education officer (with prescribed minimum qualifications and experience including as soon as possible in future a recognised professional qualification in educational administration) and define more clearly his responsibilities and powers for 'operational' as distinct from 'policy' matters in relation both to elected members and (in the case of multi-purpose LEAs) other chief officers;

6 re-affirm the statutory obligation on the Secretary of State to establish and maintain an expert Central Advisory Council with a

number of standing as well as *ad hoc* committees (the standing committees to include at the very least primary/middle, fourteen to nineteen, special educational needs, teacher training and assessment, ongoing education and training);

7   redefine in precise and comprehensive terms the national objectives and responsibility for provision of education, training and counselling for the whole fourteen to nineteen age group (or even perhaps fourteen to twenty-one), in such a way that every such young person will be recognised as a national trainee committed (full-time or in a variety of part-time modes) to education, training, work experience, community service or national service, and receiving basic payments from a rationalised national system of grants and allowances. This would mean quite simply that no young person under nineteen (or twenty-one) would be on the competitive labour market and none would be subjected to the degradation of being jobless or paid for doing nothing. How much such a scheme would cost beyond what is being spent already in various less effective ways is debatable but whatever it cost, it would be worth it.

8   re-affirm the national commitment to the provision of pre-school educational opportunities for all children under five.

That might provide a new flagship that the big and little ships of the educational world would be proud and happy to sail under!

A General Teaching Council

In her 1985 BBC/TV Dimbleby Memorial Lecture, Baroness Warnock[13] suggested four things that would greatly contribute towards the improvement of the education service. They were: the establishment of a single professional General Teaching Council analogous to the General Medical Council to set professional standards and influence teacher recruitment and training and curricular matters; greater involvement by first-rate schools and practising teachers in initial and in-service teacher training; assessment of teacher competence and effectiveness by the teaching profession itself; and a salary structure which would provide better incentives and higher rewards for top quality teachers. Few education officers in my judgement would disagree with her. The idea of a General Teaching Council has been around for a long time but, like the mirage in the desert, always seems to disappear as soon as people get close to it. However, the latest efforts of a working party of representatives of teachers' organisations under the chairmanship of John Sayer seems to have a marginally better chance of success, and it would certainly be a big step forward if the teachers could agree to establish an effective professional governing body of this kind with appropriate safeguards. Such a body might well replace the now defunct Advisory Council for the Supply and Education of Teachers and possibly also the Council for the Accreditation of Teacher Education. It could become a key element in a new, forward-looking partnership. It would (presumably) not be concerned with salary negotiations and conditions of service, but would clearly have a major contribution to make in broader 'educational' as well as narrower 'professional' matters. It is much to be hoped that it will not prove a mirage yet again.

A single, effective, national voice for local education authorities

It is my very clear and long-held view that the arrangements for a healthy education partnership in future will not be complete and satisfactory unless, in addition to a General Teaching Council and a Society of Education Officers, there is at national level an organisation comparable to the former AEC, combining the elected education leaders of LEAs and their education officers in equal membership, and able to speak for the whole education service from the LEA point of view. Without such a body the new partnership will inevitably be overweighted in favour of central government on the one hand and the teachers on the other. It should, of course, be no problem to create such an association if new single-purpose education authorities are created, but it will be much more difficult if multi-purpose unitary authorities with responsibility for education are established or if things are left (God forbid!) as they are. Nevertheless, it will be very unwise of future local education authorities, whatever form they may have, not to take urgent steps to provide themselves with one effective national organisation to embody, express and defend their share of the education partnership.

Conclusion

Just as the legitimacy of democratic government at any level derives from the consent, explicit or implicit, of the people, so the machinery of government exists to serve the people. Local government exists to support and nourish the services it provides, not the other way round. And just as local government may be destroyed by internal divisions and increasing indifference to the true needs of local communities, so it can be destroyed from the outside. If central government denies to the local authorities which it has created the discretion in decision-making required to justify their existence and the essential resources necessary to perform the tasks for which they have been made responsible; if professional and other workers within local government progressively withdraw their goodwill and increasingly disrupt local services; and if local communities react with indifference or hostility to what they see as the antics of local politicians who can neither keep the rates from rocketing nor standards of services from declining, then surely local government is doomed. The next questions, following Tim Brighouse,[14] are: 'Does it matter?' and 'What's to be done?' The argument developed in this commentary is that it would matter a lot not only to the education service but to our whole way of life, and that there is a great deal that can be done if enough of us see the dangers and take steps early enough to avoid them.

Education is a very special public service with unique needs and a unique contribution to make. In our kind of society, it has a clear duty to embody, express and teach certain basic principles (respect for other people, respect for truth, respect for democracy, respect for law, respect for the natural world)[15] but, that said, it is concerned with reconciling opposites and striking a precarious and shifting balance between the impossible extremes (freedom and discipline; individuality and conformity; innovation and tradition; leisure and work; adventure and security; equality and excellence; participation and leadership; and so on). Thus, it cannot ever be wholly 'right' and it cannot even remain acceptably 'right' in everybody's judgement for long. Moreover, it cannot, except in a thoroughly perverted form, be a satisfactory instrument for party political indoctrination and it cannot live happily in a situation which subjects it continuously to the harsher pressures of party political confrontation. It is by its very nature concerned with balance and partnership, and that is why in political terms it needs a wide measure of consensus and an accepted, stable partnership based on a genuine division of power.

In the 1950s and 1960s, most LEA education officers, I guess, would have expressed themselves reasonably content with the relationships within their authorities and with DES officials and HM Inspectors, and many like myself would have wished to express their profound gratitude for the understanding, support and friendship they received from all three sources. Very few education officers would then have questioned the division of powers/partnership approach as the proper system or the LEAs as the natural 'home' for the education service. Even today the vast majority would wish to see the essential features of the system preserved but few would deny the urgent need to improve relationships, raise standards, and restore confidence and mutual respect within the service and throughout the community.

At present many things look and feel wrong, and many things are wrong in education, but that is no reason to end on a pessimistic note. No modern nation can be civilised and prosperous for long without a highly efficient, highly regarded and highly resourced public education service. A privileged education for the few will no longer suffice; nor will a drab egalitarianism which stifles initiative and fails to nourish exceptional talent or exceptional need. Without good education for all, investment in defence, law and order, government bureaucracy, even economic productivity is ultimately sterile and self-defeating. We simply cannot afford not to have the best possible education system from pre-school to university and beyond because therein lies our hope for our own and our children's future. Sooner or later, the nation and its leaders will come back to this simple understanding and accept its implications. And meanwhile, as every education officer knows and as the Schools Curriculum Award first introduced by SEO and the journal *Education* in 1982–84 has clearly shown, there are still on the ground very many good things that go largely unremarked in the great world. We do know about and can recognise quality in education and, strange as it may seem to our critics, we still have something to teach as well as a lot to learn from the rest of the world. True, we have not mastered the art of making bricks without straw, squaring the circle or converting best practice into universal practice, and if there is a hitherto undiscovered short cut to those objectives we would all be glad to be told. But there are still a very large number of competent and dedicated people in the education service, and –

surprisingly perhaps, in view of the obvious and increasing disin-
centives – the newest recruits both to teaching and administration
seem generally to be of remarkably high quality. In them lies our
hope and because of them we must continue to fight.

But let no-one underestimate the problems and perils of the years
ahead. The dangers are avoidable and the faults remediable. But
there are many evil people and evil influences about in the world,
with more money and more power to debauch and destroy than ever
before. The education service alone cannot win the battle against
them; but without education it cannot ever be won.

It is a characteristic of the older men and women of the tribe in all
ages that they should be *laudatores temporis acti*, lamenting the present state of things and yearning ineffectively for the glad confident
morning of their youth. Certainly, many of us who were privileged
to serve in the armed forces during the war and in education during
the early post-war years of reconstruction and expansion would like
to see more evidence in our country today of the unity, commitment
and comradeship, the sense of common purpose and common
sacrifice, that most of us, younger and older, felt in those faraway
days. Of course, it is futile just to look back. The world has moved
on very fast in recent years, so fast that the 1940s and 1950s now
seem in many ways unbelievably innocent and unsophisticated. In
our modern high technology culture, there is less room than ever for
the wisdom of experience. But underneath it all, the fundamental
needs of mankind have not changed so much and go far beyond mere
physical satisfaction and material advantage. It is still as true as it
ever was that where there is no vision the people perish. And the
most powerful instrument by which to move closer to a nobler vision
for all the people is still and will always be education.

References

1   Jones G W and Stewart J D: op. cit., espec. pps. 149 and 159.
2   Tomlinson J R G: op. cit.
3   Association of Directors of Education in Scotland: *The First Twenty-
    Five Years, 1920–1945* – ADES, 1970.
4   Davies A in *Education*, Vol. 153, No. 26, June 1979, p. 743.
5   Davies A in letter to the writer, Feb. 1985.
6   Howell D: *Corporate Management in English Local Government and the*

Education Service – An Interim Report in the *Journal of Educational Administration*, Vol. XVII, No. 2, Oct. 1979, p. 223.
7   Alexander, A: op. cit., p. 173.
8   Bush T and Kogan, M: *Directors of Education* (Allen and Unwin, 1982).
9   Committee of Inquiry into the Conduct of Local Authority Business (the Widdicombe Committee) – Evidence presented by the Society of Education Officers, 1985.
10 Aldrich R and Leighton P: *Education: Time for a New Act* (Bedford Way Papers 23, London University Institute of Education, distributed by Heinemann Educational Books, 1985).
11 Cunningham, I G in *Education*, Vol. 165, No. 18, May 1985, p. 404.
12 Morris R in *Education*, Vol. 165, No. 26, June 1985, pps. 581–2.
13 Warnock Baroness: *Teacher, teach thyself* (the 1985 Richard Dimbleby Lecture) published in *The Listener*, 28th March 1985, pps. 10 to 14.
14 Brighouse T in *Education*, Vol. 165, No. 6, Feb. 1985, p. 129.
15 Cooke G V: – SEO Presidential Address, Jan. 1975.

General Index